'I don't stick with me, who will?'

The challenges and rewards of foster care

Edited by
Henrietta Bond

ADOPTION
& FOSTERING

D1321776

Published by
British Association for Adoption & Fostering
(BAAF)
Skyline House
200 Union Street
London SE1 0LX
www.baaf.org.uk

Charity registration 275689

© The collection, Introduction and Afterword Henrietta Bond, 2005

British Library Cataloguing in Publication Data
A catalogue reference record for this book is available from the
British Library

ISBN 1 903699 68 1

Project management by Jo Francis, BAAF
Photograph on cover posed by models
by Harry Cutting Photography Inc.
Designed by Andrew Haig & Associates
Typeset by Avon DataSet Ltd, Bidford on Avon, Warwickshire
Printed by Creative Print and Design, Harmondsworth

Trade distribution by Turnaround Publisher Services, Unit 3,
Olympia Trading Estate, Coburg Road, London N22 6TZ

BAAF Adoption & Fostering is the leading UK-wide membership
organisation for all those concerned with adoption, fostering and
child care.

Contents

Note about the editor

Henrietta Bond is a freelance journalist and media consultant, specialising in children and family issues. Her interest in looked after children began when she became BAAF's press officer in 1990, and since becoming freelance in 1995, she has worked with Fostering Network, The Who Cares? Trust, NCH, Barnardo's, TalkAdoption, A National Voice, and many other children and young people's organisations, and local authorities. She has written for *Guardian Society*, *Community Care*, *Care and Health*, *Children Now* and *Young People Now*. She recently authored *Fostering a Child* and a revision of the Advice Note, *Fostering: Some questions answered* for BAAF.

Acknowledgements

Many people have helped with putting together this book. First and foremost I want to thank all the amazing foster carers who gave up their time to speak to me, and the children and young people who also volunteered their comments and experiences for this book. These include Sally and Mark Betterton; Steve and Sherree Butler; Therese Cannon; Sylvia Godfrey; Annabelle Hoggan; Vaughan and Sian Jenkins; Jacqueline Mason; Tim Seward and John Vaughan; and Abrehet Tsegai.

I was also fortunate to receive the help of a number of agencies who assisted me in locating some of the carers, or who supported carers in sharing their stories with me. These include Fostering Network, TACT, Fosterplus, Barnardo's, NCH, Ryan Foster Care, PACT and The Albert Kennedy Trust.

Thanks also to Hedi Argent and Brian Cairns for their valuable comments on my first draft. I am sure that, along the line, someone has been left off this list – simply because there were so many different organisations involved. I apologise now for any omissions and hope anyone who does not see their name here will accept my apologies – and my gratitude for their help. Without so much positive support from so many people, this book could never have happened.

General note on confidentiality
The names of many of the carers, children and young people in this book have been changed for reasons of confidentiality.

Henrietta Bond
February 2005

BAAF would like to acknowledge and thank CareVisions Group for their support for this publication.

CareVisions
GROUP
Improved Outcomes for Children

www.carevisions.co.uk

Introduction

This is a book about what it really means to foster. It is an anthology of first-person experiences of foster carers who tell the true stories of children and young people they have cared for. It is about fostering in the raw, because it pulls no punches. It aims to show the problems, dilemmas, challenges, disappointments and heartbreaks that foster carers face, as well as their successes, triumphs and rewards.

The anthology set out to tell the stories of "complex" forms of foster care. It aimed to show some of the more demanding areas of work and the skills that foster carers develop to deal with these; to focus on "difficult" areas such as dealing with disclosures about sexual abuse; looking after children with HIV, or a severe disability, or Foetal Alcohol Syndrome; helping young people whose behaviour was deemed "out of control". It was intrinsically designed to be a book about fostering that would inspire and motivate new or existing carers to take on new or more challenging types of foster care. But as foster carers began to tell their stories, it became obvious that this book would have a life on several levels. Not only does it show the considerable – and at times quite amazing – range of skills carers have developed and applied to their work, but it also uncovers the many personal challenges they face which impact on their lives as individuals and family members.

Any reader hoping for a "happy" outcome to every story will be disappointed. Whilst there are some obvious success stories in this anthology, there are also stories which end painfully – when the foster carer felt betrayed by the system or, at times, betrayed by the children or young people themselves. This book does not blanch at describing several cases of allegations made by young people against their carers, or incidents where carers felt children were "wrong-footed" by social workers who failed to prioritise their needs. It looks at issues around separation and loss, which can impact as much on carers as on the children they care for. It also explores the impact of living 24 hours a day with children so traumatised by their experiences that their carers' own lives can be at risk of being overwhelmed by their child's pain.

Yet what is clear in all these stories is that an important factor in fostering is the ability to maintain a sense of proportion, to hold realistic expectations and be able to see the positives among the negatives. Not one of the carers who felt that the outcome of a child's placement was not as they would have wished it has given up fostering. All of them have dusted themselves down, evaluated the good things they felt the child gained from the placement, and then re-focused their energies on working with new children and families. In many ways this book is a testimony to the incredible strength of character and sense of commitment of highly skilled foster carers. This is also what the title of this book is all about. The title was a message that was frequently reiterated – in different words and expressions according to the individual – which then became the overriding concept for this book. If it wasn't for the dedication, commitment and sheer "stickability" of these amazing foster carers, many very troubled children and young people would have no one to support them, and no one to depend on.

| **How this book came about**

This book was commissioned by BAAF to tell the stories of individual foster carers looking after children with complex needs. A small "advert" was placed on the BAAF and Fostering Network websites as well as in some of the social care press. This asked foster carers who felt they fitted the category – and were willing to talk abut their experiences – to contact the editor. There was also a request that wherever possible the voices of the children and young people involved should be included. I then interviewed these respondents over the telephone to ascertain whether their experiences were appropriate, and to ensure that there was not too much duplication of issues between the various accounts.

From these early responses a number of stories were chosen.
However, some gaps were also identified in the process: for
example, there were no stories of carers looking after asylum
seekers. A selection of specialist fostering agencies were contacted
in the hope of identifying carers specialising in this particular area
of foster care. The remaining chapters of the book were chosen from
the contacts gained in this way.

Wherever possible, a broad geographical mix of carers from across
the UK were chosen but, because of issues of confidentiality, some
carers have chosen for their location to be moved or included under
a very general heading such as south Wales or the north of England.

When there were two carers in a family, the author tried to include
the views of both partners. However, the nature of fostering often
made it very difficult for both partners to be available at the same
time, so it was accepted that in most cases only one partner would
share their experiences.

The interviews for the chapters were conducted face-to-face or, in a
few cases, through a lengthy telephone conversation, after which I
wrote up the interview. As the chapters consist of the carers'
personal stories, the draft chapter was sent to the carer for their
approval and for them to make any amendments they felt were
necessary.

The chapters for the book were read by two external social work
professionals to ensure that the content reflected a breadth of
experience, encouraged good practice in fostering, and did not
include any material which might condone or encourage poor or
inappropriate practice.

⏐ Personal stories

The stories in this book are the experiences of carers seen through
their eyes. They are by nature subjective, and unashamedly so. They
show the situation as the carer perceived it, and what was important
to the carer in a particular situation. Carers talk about the difficulties

affecting the children and young people, the care issues or behavioural problems they faced as foster carers, their relationships with birth parents and with social workers, and their relationship with the child or young person. They explain the methods they used to work with these children but also speak about their feelings and experiences and the way they coped personally with the challenges they encountered.

This book has taken carers' stories at face value, because this is the only way such a book of first-person experiences can be written. A reader may feel that they would have done something differently, or may wonder whether the carer's perception of the situation is the "full picture", especially when carers are critical of the way social workers or other professionals handled a situation. But it is not the role of this book to take an overview of the entire situation – to do this would involve an "enquiry", and would be an altogether different piece of work.

In each chapter I have tried to capture the personality and speech patterns of the carer telling their story. Efforts have been made to retain the colloquialisms they use, and their choice of expression for describing the child's behaviour and needs. However, the material has been structured to provide an accessible read and is not quoted verbatim. In all cases carers have checked and approved the chapter after it was written.

| **Confidentiality issues**

It was recognised early on this project that it would be impossible to seek permission from all parties involved in these fostering situations before including a chapter in this book. Some of the carers are no longer involved with the children and birth families they speak about; some have ceased to work for the agency involved; and some have lost touch with the child or young person. In a book which focuses on complex fostering situations – by definition involving children with very challenging behaviour, difficult relationships between carers and birth families, and times when carers and their agency may not have seen eye-to-eye on a particular problem – to have included only stories where everyone involved (birth families, social workers, other foster carers and relevant professionals) gave full permission for a story to be included would have meant that few – if any – of these chapters could have been used.

For this reason, care has been taken to disguise both the identity of the carer but also to change names and particularly distinguishing details of children and young people. It was for this (among other reasons) that carers were sent a draft copy of their chapter and invited to consider any implications around confidentiality. Carers struggled with the need to provide an "honest" and helpful account of their experiences, which by necessity required some inclusion of the individual child or young person's circumstances, personality and behaviours, whilst not wanting to breach confidentiality. In one case, the carer felt this issue could not be resolved and decided to withdraw from the book. Some of the carers discussed the chapters with their social workers and their agencies before giving their permission for the chapter to be used.

For the purpose of ensuring confidentiality, some distinguishing details have been changed in most stories. For example, a child who came into foster care with a sibling was often described as though placed alone (unless there were significant issues about the relationship between the siblings); grandparents were turned into aunts and birth families "moved" from Edinburgh to Cardiff. Details of the foster carers' own families were also changed in some cases, as was information about other foster children living in the family. In all cases, the aim of this was to enable the carer to speak openly about the issues they encountered in caring for specific children by changing some minor details which would throw a reader "off the scent" in order to preserve confidentiality.

In each case, however, the author highlighted and discussed the issues and implications with the carers, and left the ultimate decision with the carer as to how much detail they felt should be changed. Decisions about how much was changed or left unchanged were often based on the status of the child in the family: for example, if the carer had adopted the child; if the young person was living independently and was able to express their own views; and if the carer wanted to include a story because of the important issues it raised, but had lost touch with the child concerned.

Children and young people

At the outset, the aim was to include the views of children and young people in every chapter. In Chapter 2, Michael talks very positively about his relationship with his carer. Chapter 1 involves a discussion with the children and young people and their carer. However, in the majority of cases I have, regretfully, been unable to include children's voices.

At an early stage, I realised that the book's focus on particularly complex foster care issues would limit the number of children and young people able or willing to participate. The nature of their disability or their behavioural issues meant that it was not possible to speak to some of these children. Sometimes agencies have a policy of allowing carers to speak, but wish to protect the confidentiality of the young people and so turned down a request to speak to them. In some cases, young people living independently were invited to participate by the carer and chose not to do so, but gave their permission for the carer to tell their story and saw copies of the draft chapter. For some young people, especially asylum seekers, there were issues around language but also a fear of speaking to a stranger, now that they were living in the UK as adults.

The timings of visits to carers also meant that children and young people were often at school during the interview. However, I met some of the children and young people involved in the stories and found this a very helpful and enlightening experience. Even when it was not possible to include their words, I tried to ensure that the child or young person's personality and needs were appropriately conveyed in the chapter. Meeting children who were engaging, endearing and – it has to be said – often on their "best behaviour" was a salient reminder that every child has many positive aspects to their personality. No child should be seen as the sum of their problems, but as a unique personality who deserves the very best that foster care can offer them. It was also a helpful reminder of why their carers, who may have experienced major challenges, rejections and in some cases physical assaults, still choose to continue caring for their children.

| Good practice issues

These stories are told from the carers' points of view, so the details given of how the carer handled a situation, and their relationship with other professionals, is the carer's own description. It should be borne in mind that some carers were more articulate than others, and some were more analytical and clearly identify the childcare techniques they use. However, some were more instinctive in their methods and did not always recognise the skills they brought to the task. Carers who told me that they did not think they were particularly good foster carers were often the ones who had been recommended or highly praised by their agencies. Carers also tended to be reflective, and keen to learn and to do an even better job in the future. They were often honest about their perceived mistakes and as willing to talk about what hadn't worked as what had worked. This means that there is a selection of experiences in the book, of carers describing practices that they felt worked well but also describing incidents where they felt that things could have been handled better, either by themselves or by others they were working with.

Hopefully there are no incidents in this book which could be considered "bad practice". However, some methods may appear a little unorthodox, and are often the result of a carer having tried everything else they – or their social workers – could think of! In some cases, carers only describe one aspect of a way of working, and may not give the full picture, not explaining that they are drawing on a wealth of training and experience. One carer, reading the draft of her chapter, felt that in her own words she had made her practices sound rather "harsh". When she explained this concern to me, it became clear that the methods she was following were part of a behavioural programme devised by a psychologist and endorsed by her agency. The carer, the carer's social worker and I were then able to discuss how these working methods could be explained by the carer in a slightly different context, which would make them more understandable to the reader.

Readers may notice that some carers make little or no reference to other professionals. In some cases this was simply because the carer and the social worker knew each other so well that it almost went without saying that the foster carer had a long-standing, supportive relationship with their support worker or the child's worker, who would regularly discuss with them the way they worked with the child or young person. Some carers chose to commend their social workers or to give particular mention to a school teacher or health professional they perceived as very helpful. However, in some cases the carers quite clearly felt unsupported by social workers and other professionals. Some carers actively criticised what they felt was poor practice on the part of the agency or other professionals they were working with. It is not the purpose of this book to explore what actually happened or did not happen in these situations, but to convey the carer's personal view of how this impacted on them, as the person caring for the child or young person.

| Safe care

There are several mentions of "safe care" in this book, but there are also mentions of the importance of warmth and physical contact between carers and the children they cared for. This represents the dilemma many carers face around ensuring that they protect the child from situations that could be perceived as abusive, and protect themselves from allegations of abuse, whilst wanting to make the child or young person feel as much a "normal" part of the family as possible, and encourage emotional growth and understanding of safe, positive physical contact.

Most carers who tell their story in this book mention their foster children seeking or receiving physical affection from their carers. They also mention children giving their carers hugs or kisses. Some explain this in the context of a long-term relationship with the child and a build-up of trust and mutual respect. Some mention it without giving a broader context. However, all the carers interviewed were very aware of the issues raised by physical contact, and some particularly asked for things to be carefully worded so that innocent actions could not be misinterpreted.

From interviewing carers for this book it became clear that positive physical contact with foster children is offered on the child's terms, that children's personal space is respected and the child is offered opportunities for appropriate gestures of affection, or soothing contact such as foot or hand massages, but this is never imposed or forced upon the child. It is with this understanding that all passing – rather than detailed – mentions of physical contact are included. All mentions of physical affection were included on the understanding by the author that this can be an important part of establishing a child's self-esteem and helping them to express emotions, develop relationship skills and increase their understanding of what is and is not appropriate behaviour.

Some carers also mention using some forms of physical restraint for the safety of the child, for example, holding a child who is about to run out into the road or hurt themselves or someone else, or confining a child to a limited area. It should be remembered that some of the children described in this book have quite extreme behavioural issues and that there are times when a carer may need to use some form of appropriate restraint to prevent the child endangering themselves or others. Carers often spoke about having discussed these methods of restraint with their social workers, or of seeking permission to lock doors or windows to prevent the child endangering or hurting themselves.

| The stories

Chapter 1: Annabelle and family

This chapter documents a discussion between a foster carer and the three young women she has fostered, all of whom have been affected by sexual abuse. The account focuses on the young people's very different types of challenging behaviour and how Annabelle has helped them to restore their self-confidence, learn to express their feelings and to become accepted and valued members of their local community.

Chapter 2: Debra and Michael

The story of a long-term carer for a boy with HIV, this chapter examines how other people's prejudices forced Debra and her family to move house. It considers the medical and confidentiality issues surrounding the care of a child with HIV, but shows the many rewards of looking after a young person who is intelligent, outgoing, sensitive and affectionate.

Chapter 3: Julie and Jason

This chapter tells the story of a mixed-heritage couple helping a very distressed, mixed-heritage child with mild autism to come to terms with separation from his birth mother and previous foster carer, and to gain an understanding of his own identity. The little boy's confusion presents itself in very difficult behaviour which Julie has learnt different ways to manage. The chapter also includes issues around working with parents and "learning to let go" when children return home or are adopted.

Chapter 4: Philip and Roger

This account includes a variety of experiences of caring for Albanian boys, and the problems of crossing language and cultural divides. Philip explains how developing trust between carer and child helped to make some placements very successful, as well as the difficulties of fostering adolescents whose traumatic pasts and experiences of self-reliance can make it hard for them to accept the care of an adult.

Chapter 5: Kathy and Francis

Their experience of looking after a child with learning difficulties who had been abused caused Kathy and Francis to consider whether fostering was right for them. However, the couple have since fostered girls with traumatic pasts and attachment difficulties, manifested in a range of behaviours including temper tantrums and physical aggression. The couple explain how they work as a team and which methods they use to modify challenging behaviour and build up the girls' self-esteem.

Chapter 6: Jabeen and Hussain

This chapter looks at how a family have long-term fostered an "institutionalised" teenage boy with severe learning difficulties and behaviour problems. Jabeen explains the methods they have used to help the boy express his feelings and overcome his aggressive behaviours. She describes how he has learnt to fit into a home environment and how they have helped him control his behaviour so that he can go out into the community.

Chapter 7: Robin and Louise

A couple who foster as a partnership describe their experiences of caring for four severely neglected children, who eventually returned to their own family. Robin explains how the couple helped these siblings to develop their self-esteem and to learn how to be "children", and the outcomes for each of them. He describes the difficulties of working with the children's birth mother, and the challenges carers face when supporting children through changes which they feel may not be in the child's best interests.

Chapter 8: Clive and Iain

A couple describe their experience of providing supported lodgings to a vulnerable, homeless young man with learning difficulties. They consider the impact of having a young adult living in their home and the lessons they have learnt from this, as well as how they have worked to help him develop social skills and appropriate behaviour, and to prepare for "independent" living.

Chapter 9: Abi and Fatmir
This chapter describes the experience of caring for an asylum-seeking child, by looking at how an Eritrean foster carer integrated a young man from Eastern Europe into her family, by adapting her own home to the young person's needs. It shows how she overcame language and cultural divides through her shared understanding of how it feels to be a "refugee". This chapter also examines the young person's behavioural problems and the decisions Abi made to help him work through these.

Chapter 10: Maud, Nathan and Leo
This chapter describes how a single carer has looked after two boys with Foetal Alcohol Syndrome and Foetal Alcohol Effects, and the major impact this has had on her life. Maud explains how these conditions damage a child's brain development and cause impulsive, reckless behaviour which other people perceive as anti-social or even criminal. She highlights the need for good support and for better public understanding of the effects of alcohol on the unborn child.

Chapter 11: Vaughan and Sian
In this account, Vaughan describes how he and his partner fostered a damaged but delightful young man with learning difficulties and sexualised behaviour. He explains the ways in which the family managed to contain these behaviours and the progress this young man made while living with them. Vaughan also describes his sadness about the way the placement disrupted after the young man made false allegations, but how important it is to focus on the positive things they are able to offer children in their care.

Chapter 12: Therese and Joanne
This chapter describes how a foster carer worked with a young woman from secure accommodation to help her to reintegrate into the community. Therese describes the techniques she used for managing the girl's challenging behaviour and tendency to abscond, how she helped this young woman to cope with major experiences of grief and separation, and how she dealt with her own feelings when the young woman chose to move out.

These stories are very different. Every child is unique and has their own distinctive needs. Every carer is an individual and has their own way of working, even when drawing on ideas provided through training or discussion with other professionals. However, what is consistent between each chapter is the enormous level of commitment, determination and perseverance shown by these carers in finding ways to help the child cope with past problems and move forward. Coupled with this is an underlying respect for the children and young people, compassion for the difficulties both they and their families have experienced, and a sense of pride, and admiration for everything these children have achieved.

Henrietta Bond
February 2005

Annabelle and her family: Living with the hurts from the past

There is no panacea for the hurts that sexually and emotionally abused children have suffered, according to experienced foster carer Annabelle. She believes that time, patience and finding out what motivates each individual is the only way to start the process of helping a traumatised child cope with their past experiences and rebuild trust in the adults around them.

Together with support from her mother, Janet, single carer Annabelle from the north of England has cared for three girls who have all experienced abuse and neglect in their early lives. Annabelle fostered, then adopted, Zoe (20), has a residence order for Chantelle (12) and is long-term fostering Louise (11). Annabelle is a qualified social worker. She fosters for her local authority.

Annabelle tells the family's story, together with her adopted daughter Zoe. The two younger children arrived home from school during this time and joined the conversation for a while.

Annabelle: I was 29 with no man on the horizon and I knew I wanted children in my life. I'd worked in youth clubs and nurseries, been a nanny, and worked with children in my role as a social worker. What I did know was that I didn't want a baby. I approached Barnardo's in the early 1980s, when single carers were much less common. I was approved by them and waiting for a child to be placed when I saw Zoe in BAAF's *Be My Parent* newspaper. She was described as 'bright and cheerful, but could be very challenging'.

Apparently Zoe's previous foster placements had broken down because carers had found her behaviour 'too wearing'. Because of the abuse she'd experienced, Zoe found it hard to be around men. She had been well prepared for her move to me by her experienced foster carers, which was helpful. Zoe was almost eight when she first came to live with me. She was placed for fostering, with a view to adoption.

Zoe: I read through my notes the other day. They said that I was really looking forward to a new family. Apparently I'd moved 17 times between 25 different placements by the time I was five. My mother had post-natal depression and my dad was schizophrenic. My mum spiralled into illness very quickly and when I did go home my dad was the main caregiver. I know I was naughtier and naughtier every time I went back to my family because it was another disruption to my stability.

My dad abused me when I was about three. He was later charged and convicted. My earliest memories are of that abuse. I'd spent time in a specialist residential child psychology unit. I know I was very confused. I know that the psychology unit had helped me put some of the pieces of the jigsaw in place and I remember being able to relate to people and get on with them better. But I was anxious all the time. I also found it hard that my brother was living with my mother, because he did a lot of caring for her. I felt I was always put in foster care because of the way I behaved. It shouldn't be like that for any child. But I'm lucky, I've been compensated for those bad times with the good memories I now have of growing up in this family.

Annabelle: I know they say every child has a "honeymoon" period when they first move in – but I'm still waiting! Zoe's behaviour was challenging from the start. Although Zoe was initially a foster placement, I felt I'd committed to her and right or wrong I was going to stick with her. Zoe had experienced so many moves and every time the social worker came to the house she freaked because she thought she was going to move again.

The big thing was getting to know each other. In some ways taking a child into your home is like a relationship with a partner. You fall in love and only afterwards do you get to know each other properly. Zoe got up in the night and roamed around the house. This went on for the first eight weeks until gradually I persuaded her to stay in her room and read or come through to me for a cuddle. It seemed that some of the abuse she'd experienced had happened at night and so nights were a difficult time for her. She had recurring nightmares about the wardrobe door opening. I changed the furniture around and that seemed to help her.

We have three rules in this house. They are: don't hurt yourself; don't hurt other people; and don't intentionally damage things. Of course, that doesn't mean that the rules always get followed! Zoe could be quite violent and had a big thing about lying. She drew on the wall and signed it "Zoe", and then said she hadn't done it. And she used to fly into rages where she'd swear and break and rip things.

Zoe: I know I was testing you out, trying to push you away. Because I thought I was going to leave you, anyway. There was so much misplaced anger inside me – Jekyll and Hyde stuff. I'd feel guilty because I'd given you such a crappy time. You'd massage my back and I'd feel I didn't deserve it.

Annabelle: You really felt you didn't deserve things. You couldn't handle praise at all at first. But you can't expect a child to have years of rubbish in their life and be able to wash it away overnight. Zoe was a great one for writing me letters. She'd send me notes that read: 'Dear Mum, I know you are downstairs with men and you are smoking. Lots of love, Zoe xxx'. My feeling was that chance would be a fine thing! But she had a real worry that I'd go off with a man and leave her.

Zoe: I was so jealous of anyone having Mum's attention. My mum had a lovely male friend – just a friend, but I felt very threatened by that friendship. I think it took me five years to realise that she was going to stick with me.

Annabelle: I think what worked in the relationship with Zoe was having good routines. But also I'm a great believer that children should be doing lots of different activities, so they can find things they're good at. Zoe went horse riding and loved art and drawing. She was very good at swimming. That helped to build her self-confidence. And Zoe discovered a talent for archery. We'd go all over the country in our tent so she could compete. It was wonderful seeing her getting medals for archery and realising she'd gone from being an underachiever to an achiever. And it helped her to realise that adults had respect for her. She started doing better at school as well. I remember the headteacher was very impressed by Zoe's caring nature. I bring up all my children to believe that beauty on the inside is greater than beauty on the outside. Zoe left school with nine GCSEs and she's now training to be a nurse.

Zoe: I was always a large child and I got teased about it. Annabelle helped me deal with that. There are many things you have to deal with after sexual abuse. It's about redefining your boundaries and reclaiming your body. My mum and my gran helped me to have a sense of myself, to appreciate that my body was my own. Gran lives with us and she's strict but very fair. I was able to talk to them both, and that really helped.

Annabelle: I wanted Zoe to have contact with her own mum and her previous foster carers. You can feel a bit jealous but you have to recognise that you're the adult in this situation and you have to do what is best for the child. Zoe's mum died when she was 13. I'd have hated it if she hadn't had the chance to know her properly beforehand. When Zoe's mum was ill, Zoe went down to our local church to pray. She put in the visiting book that her mum was dying. I got a surprise from the vicar's wife who thought I'd suddenly been taken very ill . . . But it was lovely that Zoe wanted to do that, and took the initiative herself.

Zoe: My mum was moved to a specialist unit and Annabelle came with me to visit her. I always felt that Annabelle loved her as much as I did. If there was an animosity, I didn't ever feel it. I think Annabelle handled the situation brilliantly.

Annabelle: Zoe's mum once said to me, 'I really love you'. I think she was trying to tell me that she was pleased that Zoe was OK with me. I adopted Zoe after fostering her for a year. By then we all felt it was the right thing to do. For each of my children I try to give them what they need as individuals. Some children need the security of knowing they are legally part of your family, others don't need that. Again, it's like a relationship with a partner. Some couples want marriage, but some are just as happy to live together. Chantelle was fostered for nearly five years before I applied for a Residence Order because she wanted this. Louise is currently fostered and on a Care Order. We may go for a Residence Order if that feels right for her.

As Zoe got into her teens, I started doing respite fostering and Zoe handled that very well. As a family we decided we would look at longer-term fostering. When Chantelle came to us she was six-and-a-half and the size of a three-year-old. She had a long history of neglect and physical and possible sexual abuse. Her siblings had been fostered elsewhere and she'd stayed with relatives for a while but it hadn't worked out, so she'd been moved to foster carers. She'd experienced so much rejection, she didn't trust anyone and was in emotional meltdown.

Zoe: We looked at Chantelle's papers together. I never felt excluded from anything. I was excited but also a bit threatened. Chantelle wasn't easy but I always knew I didn't want her to leave us.

Chantelle and Louise returned from school and joined the conversation at this point.

Annabelle: Zoe has done a lot to make Chantelle and Louise's placements work. She'd learnt to manage her own behaviour and she helped them to do the same. Zoe has more understanding of their situation than I'll ever have. She can get away with saying things to them that I could never say!

When Chantelle arrived she was ultra-cute and could charm the birds off the trees. But her previous foster carers had videoed her having a "paddy", and Chantelle was very good at paddys! So we knew what to expect.

Chantelle: It was my way of getting my anger out. I didn't know what to do with my feelings.

Annabelle: Chantelle used to rip her clothes to shreds. I used to strip her to her underwear if she started a paddy, otherwise I couldn't afford to clothe her! At six years old she'd done £3,000 worth of damage to the school library because someone left her alone in there to cool down! I'd know what sort of day we were going to have from the moment Chantelle got out of bed. Her tantrums could go from two to four hours at a time. Many a morning I'd carry her to the car under my arm while she yelled her head off. You had to let her release the anger but try and keep her safe while it happened. Then one day, coming home from school in the car, I said to her, 'Chuck the paddy out of the window and we'll drive very fast so it can't catch up with us.' That image seemed to help her and from then onwards she started learning how to control her anger. I think the problem was that nobody had ever said "no" to her and meant it. She had to realise that someone saying "no" didn't mean that she'd lost control of a situation or that she'd never be able to take control of situations for herself.

The other big issues were the lies she told, and taking other people's things. She'd been taught to shop-lift when she was in her pram. It was very important to have close links with the school so she couldn't tell me and the school different things. I started a little book which went between school and home. The teacher wrote down what had happened during the day. There was also a page at the back where the teacher could put in stars when she'd behaved well . . .

Chantelle: I got stars for telling the truth, not talking when the teacher talked, remembering my homework, not making faces when people weren't looking . . . for two stars I got a sweet, for five stars I could choose a video. For 20 stars I got 25p into my pocket money, 50 gold stars was a small beanie baby and 100 gold stars was a large one – 100 stars was a Sylvanian Family set.*

Annabelle: A system like that doesn't work for every child but it worked for Chantelle. Children need motivation and to see the outcome of trying to change their behaviour. With every thing they achieve, their self-esteem goes up. I think it's very important to work on getting the "outside" behaviour right as soon as you can. If you can help a child manage their behaviour so they can get through a school day, they then start to have a sense of achievement, and to be thought of well by others. And they start to make friends. I feel it's important for all my girls to be polite and help other people, because when you behave like this, people respect you and you feel valued. They know that I love them whatever they do – although I don't always like their behaviour – but they need to understand that outsiders won't automatically like them, unless they show them that they deserve to be treated with respect.

Chantelle also does a lot of activities. She plays the flute, and she's good at dancing, cheerleading and cross-country. We live in a village and it's fairly safe for children to be outdoors. I love them to come in mucky, and to know they've been out with the dogs, running around and roller-skating and letting off steam. Exercise is a great way of defusing anger. Chantelle has worked so hard to deal with her rages. She used to explode several times a day, now it's only once or twice a year.

Chantelle: I like it now that things are better.

* small woodland animal figurines.

Annabelle: Louise was eight when she came. She was such a cutie pie. She was supposed to be adopted with her brothers but the judge thought she'd be better on her own, and that made her very sad. She'd also experienced things at her previous foster carers' which weren't right . . .

Louise: I was scared of the dark. I was scared of moving. I was scared here 'cos I didn't know where everything was.

Annabelle: Louise had problems at night for the same reasons as Zoe. Also I think her social worker hadn't understood that she had learning difficulties. People thought it was failure to thrive but she was struggling with lots of things . . .

Louise: Here I feel loved a lot. When I'm really cross I say I want to leave this family. But I don't.

Annabelle: We talk about the fact that when you get angry you sometimes say things you don't mean. I've tried to help Louise see that when you behave well good things come from that . . .

Louise: To get good things you do the right things. I like to go horse riding. I like going on my bike, I like going to the beach with the dogs.

Annabelle: What are the things you are really good at, Louise?

Louise: Running and swimming.

Annabelle: Louise really struggles at maths and English. She had problems with co-ordination. She started doing gymnastics to help with her co-ordination. She found she was good at the high jump, running and swimming. I think that at first Louise felt she was the bad girl and Chantelle was the good girl. The first time Louise saw Chantelle have a paddy she stood there with her mouth open! Louise has found there are lots of things she can be good at. She does jobs around the house and she looks after her rabbit. But Louise finds change difficult. She also found it difficult to tell us how she felt. Louise had real problems with empathy but she's learnt about other people's feelings, as well as expressing her own. When my mother's budgie died, Louise showed real compassion for her. She recognised my mother's grief and hugged her. That was a very big step for her.

Chantelle and Louise left the conversation at this point to do their homework.

Annabelle: When children have experienced neglect, sexual abuse and been "scape-goated" in their birth families, they can shut down their feelings. It's so good to see feelings coming out. I'd always rather a child yells and stamps than stands around smiling inanely. It has been harder for Louise because of her learning disabilities but now we know she is affected in this way, we can help her to learn how to make the best of her life.

Because all my girls have been through sexual abuse I am very clear about safe care. There is no flaunting of bodies, no staring at nudity in this house. Between your neck and your knees you don't show anyone except the doctor. I know it sounds simplistic but you can have too many rules and too many choices, and that gets confusing for children. I've had children masturbate in the supermarket, wear the heads off dolls, and rub themselves against visitors. I say that masturbation is nothing to be ashamed of but it's for your bedroom only. I try to help them recognise situations where they feel uncomfortable, and where they might be at risk. We have lots of very frank, open discussions in this household because it's so important that these children know how to keep themselves safe. I want them to realise that healthy adult relationships are pleasurable, and I'm so pleased that Zoe is able to talk to me about boyfriends. I was so scared that, after everything my children had been through, they'd be totally mixed up.

Louise has seen some awful things being done to babies and small children, and she experienced a lot of it herself. She'd been taught to interact sexually with other children and there were problems with her trying to undress and fondle other children. Louise used to stare at my body and try to look at me undressing. I said to her, 'Do you remember when that happened to you, how you didn't like it because it made you feel uncomfortable?' so I could explain to her how I felt. We try and encourage all the children to talk openly about the things that bother them and over the years all our children have talked about their abuse. It took Louise more than a year to tell us what she had experienced. One day she just sat down on the couch and it all came out. I find that all the children seem to be able to disclose things to my mother – maybe it's because she is part of an older generation that they feel real security with her. I think the children know she is 100 per cent there for them.

We have to help Louise understand that none of this was her fault. When there are small children around we say, 'Look how small and vulnerable they are. That was how small you were when these things happened to you. Could you have done anything about it?'

Zoe: It's stability and trust that makes you able to talk about these things. If you don't have that, you don't feel safe enough to disclose. It's a big deal to tell someone you were abused and you need to know you won't be dismissed, that they will do justice to your feelings.

Annabelle: You have to make sure that children don't feel that you are shocked or disgusted by them in any way, and at the same time convey that you'd like to shoot the boots off people who have hurt them. Communication is vital. And we've been lucky that the girls' families have shared information with us about their past. My girls have had to deal with some tough stuff but they've developed the maturity to cope with it. Zoe is so good, she's more mature than many young people of her age. She's been working with dying patients in a hospice; she has the skills to do that.

Zoe: I need to be needed. But I've never once thought I can't do these things, because Annabelle has taught me to believe that I can achieve things. And I've enjoyed being involved in fostering the other girls. Annabelle has a certain strength and patience as a foster carer, as well as a very good support network.

Annabelle: I have my mum who lives with me, and my brother and sister-in-law – they are all absolutely wonderful. They have invested as much in the children as I have. But I'm also not afraid to ask for help. I may be a social worker but I'm not afraid to say if I feel we need counselling or therapy services. And I probably mishandle situations as often as I get them right.

I always say fostering is about giant steps and tiny steps, and sometimes it's the tiny steps which are the biggest achievements, like Louise being able to cry when the rabbit died, or coming to say 'I love you and I love Gran too!' And it may sound corny but I love all my girls, I just do. They are very precious and very wonderful and they've all had to cope with so much. I can only do so much but they are the ones who make the real achievements. I feel so proud of them all.

2

Debra and Michael:
A child, not a disease

**When neighbours discovered that Debra's foster
son Michael was HIV positive, the whole family
had to move to a new town. Yet Debra believes
that Michael has greatly enriched her life, and
describes him as a 'highly rewarding young
person to care for'.**

**As a white single carer who has two older sons,
Debra sees fostering as a career choice. As well
as caring for Michael full-time, Debra provides
regular respite care for sibling groups. Debra,
who lives in the south of England, has emotional
support from her male partner, but the couple
have chosen not to live together.**

Debra tells their story:

I met my foster son during a meeting in a social services office in
London. In the far corner of the room there was a man who looked
exhausted and grey, holding his son who appeared to be about two
years old. The child had the most beautiful dramatic eyes, filled with
fear and wonderment. This frail, gorgeous little boy was Michael,
who was to become part of my family.

I had originally wanted to foster an older child, perhaps a teenager
or a mother and baby but because of my background, working as a
nurse in an HIV clinic, social workers had approached me about
Michael. The social workers told me they were looking for a
placement for a child with HIV, currently living in London in
temporary foster care. His mother had died and his father, very sick
himself, had felt unable to care for the toddler. The father lived in

the south west of England, and I think everyone was very relieved to find someone to care for this child who also lived so close to his remaining family.

During our first meeting the social worker said, 'This is Debbie, the lady who will be fostering Michael'. And then she said to Michael, 'This is the lady you will be living with'. Michael looked anxious and appeared to be worried about what was going on. I spent the rest of the meeting smiling at him and playing with him to try and reassure him. We made the move to my house a gradual process. I visited him several times in London over a couple of months, and when he eventually arrived, his short-term foster carer came with him and stayed in a local bed and breakfast for a couple of days, to settle him and make sure everything went well.

It was vitally important that Michael's medication was correct, so I had to ensure that I completely understood what to do. He was connected to a feeding machine overnight as he had a very poor appetite and it was important that he put on weight. When you care for a child with a complex medical condition like HIV, it helps if you understand the nature of the condition. I knew it would be impossible to catch the condition by caring for him, but also understood that he will always be more prone to infection than other children. Illnesses like chickenpox can be very dangerous for him. A simple cough and cold can sometimes lead to a serious chest infection.

Michael's drugs gave him severe diarrhoea and tummy pains and he often vomited after his medication in those early days. I changed my carpets to wooden flooring and I would always be prepared with a mop and bucket. If he was sick straight after his medication, I had to give it to him again. Although I knew he needed these drugs to stay alive, I felt like I was poisoning him. Medication has to be given on time, often in those early days several times a day, some with food and some without, so our lives had to revolve around medication and the clean-ups afterwards. Life felt overwhelming.

Those early days were often exhausting and in the middle of it all my own son, Jack, who'd been really excited about fostering, became very clingy. Although we'd discussed taking on a new member of the family, adjusting to changes in our routines was very difficult for him, so it was important to give Jack extra attention too. It took Jack some weeks to settle down and get used to Michael being around, but these days the boys are the very best of friends.

During that time I had a message on my wall saying "24 hours at a time". I knew I could cope with anything for just one day. I was often so busy caring for Michael that my social worker would help me by doing the washing up when he visited. This was the sort of support I needed and I was very grateful to him.

Michael's mother had died six months previously and, bereaved, he would cry for her. It broke my heart to see him so unhappy and I felt helpless. I would try to explain to him that his mother had loved him very much, that she had not wanted to die but sometimes people got sick and couldn't help it. I told him she would never have wanted to leave him but I was his second mummy and I would love him just as much. Over time, as we talked, he told me he thought she had gone away in a space ship because someone had said she was in heaven, in the sky. He used to say, 'My mummy is dead but I don't know where she is or when she is coming back'. Children often have no real concept of death until they are around the age of seven.

It took many months before Michael settled, and now he says he is lucky to have had two mums, both of which have loved him so much. We often look at photographs of his mother and on special occasions we have sent helium balloons, with messages attached to them, into the sky. Last year we planted a rose for her on Mother's Day and it was so heavy with flowers this summer that I felt she must have been watching over him.

From the start Michael had regular contact with his father. His father is often unwell but it is good for Michael to see him, and it gives him stability. I think it will be very hard for Michael when his father dies; he's had so much loss in his life. Social services are happy for him to stay with me for the rest of his childhood and I hope to have the special place of his "second mum" throughout his whole life. His father is relieved that Michael is so loved and cared for.

Michael is a rewarding child to look after. He has great empathy with other people and is very caring. At the age of five he said to me, 'Sit down Mum, you look tired, I'll get you a mat for your coffee.' A year later he made me a cup of coffee for Mother's Day. He made it with cold water because he wasn't allowed to use the kettle. It was a struggle but I drank it, thanking him for his kindness.

When Michael was five he started at the local school. He knew he was ill but he didn't know the nature of his illness. Even 22 years after HIV got its name, stigma and discrimination against people with the virus continues unabated, and therefore his diagnosis was kept secret from all but those who needed to know. Living in such a rural area I felt we had to be careful or our lives could be made difficult. Government guidelines advise not telling the school, understanding that the risk of prejudice and discrimination destroys people's lives. If confidentiality is breached, it can have a detrimental psychological effect on the child but also a knock-on effect on the child's health.

Social services, however, had other ideas. In spite of overwhelming evidence that other children were not at risk and warnings from health professionals and Government guidelines about the risks of sharing that information, social services told the school. The headteacher agreed to enrol Michael, but did not cope well. In spite of her education she had trouble overcoming her fear. Many years of hysterical press articles had closed her mind and, although she agreed to keep his diagnosis a secret, a year later I discovered that she had shared our very confidential information with others, including teachers and people applying for jobs at the school. Over the next year we experienced minor breaches of confidence from social workers and health workers and I began to lose confidence in everyone.

Michael started school and quickly became popular with both children and staff. We had some silly incidents with the school, such as not wanting to take him swimming and sending him to the office if there was a sick child in class. They once taped up his mouth with Elastoplasts when his lip bled. When I complained bitterly to social services, I was told that I must excuse them because they were very frightened! If they had done that with any other child, it would have been considered an assault and those responsible would have been immediately suspended. I was not impressed!

A year after Michael started school our lives were turned upside down. Someone spoke out of turn, confidentiality was breached, a parent heard the word "AIDS" and, like a forest fire, that word spread throughout the village. The headteacher heard first and rang me, advising me not to bring Michael to school; she felt there would be a scene. I didn't have to wait long! The doorbell rang and there was a woman shouting, 'We don't want you here, he's got AIDS and we don't want you in this village'. I saw other people milling about, talking and pointing. The woman on my doorstep said people were going to a meeting to get us out of the village. She was very aggressive and I was frightened and started to cry, and just kept saying that their children were not at risk. I could not confirm or deny his HIV status, although at this point it was far too late for that.

I was terrified, my mouth was dry and I couldn't think properly but I realised as they started their meeting that it would be safer to leave. I grabbed Michael, my son Jack, and Michael's drugs and we ran to the car still wearing our nightclothes. Michael was hysterical, as he had heard everything. I was confused and frightened – everything had happened so quickly and I had nowhere to go. I stopped in the next village at the home of my electrician's mother and borrowed a long cardigan to cover my nightdress. She must have thought I had gone mad, but I asked her not to ask any questions in front of Michael and she was kind enough to comply.

We then went on to a transport café, which was the only place open so early, and I sat, still in shock, with a cup of coffee. I was shaking so badly I could not get it to my mouth. Jack was silent and white-faced, Michael was crying. Even today, years later, tears come to my eyes when I think back to that morning.

I always knew that there would be some small-minded people who would be prepared to cause us problems, but I had been unprepared for the extreme prejudice and hatred that we had faced. I was so shocked that this could lead to such panic and hostility towards a tiny, sick child. Would they have persecuted us if he had had cancer or another incurable illness? They actually believed that Michael was a risk to their children. The TV programme *Eastenders* had recently covered issues around HIV and prejudice, but blind fear and ignorance had overwhelmed these people and they did not want to hear the voice of reason. Villagers were fuelling each other's hatred and trying to justify their cruelty to a small, helpless child.

Social services arranged for us to stay at a respite centre for people with HIV and we remained there, supported and counselled by the staff for four days. The centre is normally expensive but the staff took us in for nothing because they felt so sorry for us. I was deeply grateful. My wonderful social worker collected some clothes for us from my home. I was frightened Michael would be moved away from me because social services thought the breach of confidentiality would be detrimental to his wellbeing and ability to live a normal life in our community. I begged my social worker to keep him with me because I felt that moving him to another family would be distressing for him, and even if he moved, there was no guarantee it wouldn't happen in another foster family's community. I said I would move anywhere in the country to keep him safe if that was necessary. The social worker reassured me that they would never consider moving Michael to another family because of what had happened. They knew Michael was well cared for and loved. My worker joked that I was possibly the first homeless foster carer in the country!

A few days later we returned to the village but there was a menacing silence. Health officials had been to talk to the villagers but many did not want to listen. We were ostracised. Michael was shunned, no one would play with him and although I was allowed to take him to school, I had to do so after the other parents had gone in the morning and collect him before the other children were picked up, in case of hostility. If we went to the park after school, it would empty. Mothers would stand at their front doors with crossed arms and stare as we walked by. One day someone called out, 'He should have been put down at birth!' Can you imagine how anyone could shout that at a child? The girls who lived opposite us told us they were not allowed to play with Michael. Even my own son's friends stopped coming round to play. I felt that we were being treated like lepers in the Middle Ages. The local newspaper heard about us and printed the headline 'AIDS boy hounded out of village'. I was shocked that they had referred to him as 'AIDS boy'. He is a child, not a disease! In response to all this, Michael would plead, 'I just want to be human like the other children'.

We decided we had little choice but to move. We arranged for the removal van to arrive very early in the morning and left as quickly as we could for a town some 50 miles away. This also proved to be a disaster because the three schools we approached over-reacted. One even threatened us with contacting the newspapers if we tried to take up a place for Michael there. They need not have bothered. *The News of the World* had already picked up our story from the local newspaper and was, to my amazement, incredibly supportive. They were angry that vigilantes had hounded this frail, beautiful little boy from his home. The journalist was horrified that he was made to feel that he was not human and said it was heartbreaking that he should feel this way. The journalist's message was very clear. Other children are NOT at risk. HIV is spread by unprotected sex, sharing syringes and blood transfusion. It was appalling that society had treated people like this, and it was time we stopped assuming that people with AIDS are bad people who deserve what they get. What had been done to this little boy should make us ashamed to be human.

A couple of years later I was to meet the editor of *The News of the World*, and told him how very grateful we were for the newspaper's support at such a difficult time in our lives. He met Michael and shook his hand and told him that he was a very special boy. No photos were taken, there were no trashy headlines to sell newspapers, this was just a very kind man who cared enough to say 'hello' to a little boy with an incurable illness.

Still dismayed by the outright ignorance expressed in HIV guidelines, and the level of prejudice in schools, I contacted the Minister for Education. He was shocked to find such small-mindedness in school staff and said this was not acceptable. He wrote again to all schools reminding them of their guidelines, although he agreed they were unenforceable in law. He suggested moving to London where, he assured me, I would not experience such stupidity and discrimination. He said that London boroughs would already have their own HIV policies in place, and we would get the support and protection that Michael obviously needed.

Moving again, we found a school with a wonderful headteacher who fully understood what we had been through, and why we needed confidentiality. In an ideal situation we would be able to talk to other parents about the virus and have their support, in the way you would expect with any child with a life-limiting condition. However, because of the extreme over-reaction of some families, this is not possible. Confidentiality is of the utmost importance to protect these children and keep them safe. They learn very quickly the need for secrecy about their illness, and families affected by the disease live in secrecy and isolation. Yet they are the families that most need support and help.

It's strange how little people know about HIV. These days medication is so good that the level of virus in Michael's blood is undetectable. Newspaper articles in the 1980s scaremongered, and I suppose that sort of article sells many more newspapers than writing about the common sense information so desperately needed by the public today.

Michael is now 12 years old and in the first year at his secondary school. He is still very thin and finds sports a struggle as he gets very tired, but he is an exceptional boy who enjoys computers, art and drama. He has settled well in our new home and has lots of friends in school and in our neighbourhood. In every school report teachers comment on how cheerful and kind he is and what a pleasure he is to have in class. I've tried not to spoil him, but then again it would be difficult to do that because he is always so considerate and has so much empathy for other people and their feelings. He has bags of personality and is quite a performer!

Because Michael is very mature for his age, we often talk about things together. When I explained what was wrong with him, he took the news calmly and bravely. He says he has decided to dedicate his life to trying to help educate people about HIV, to dispel fear and ensure that no other sick child has to be hurt by ignorance and prejudice. Michael recently won a Child of the Year award for his courage, and the presenter asked him how he felt when people treated him badly. His reply was, 'Like something out of the rubbish'. I try to counterbalance those feelings by showing him how much he is loved and wanted. I say to him that he is gifted and special, and perhaps he has been given the opportunity to make a difference, to change people's attitudes. He tells me that people only say stupid things about HIV and AIDS because they are afraid.

Often Michael has said that he would like to go on television and talk about living with his illness, but I tell him he must wait until he is older. Whilst he is young it is my duty to think through the consequences and try to protect him as well as I can. He knows that at the moment he has to keep his diagnosis secret and understands why that is so. He has helped me write his story here so that other people can understand that there is no need to be frightened of him – that he is just a normal little boy.

It has been hard for me to form friendships and relationships with other people because I am always aware that the same things could happen again. I am often unwilling to have friends into my home in case I have inadvertently left any paperwork around and they might discover our secret. My current partner is very committed to Michael and treats him like a son, and if our relationship ends, I know he would never put us at risk. He is a wonderful person and a great support to me.

Michael's prognosis changes all the time with improved medication and specialist care. We have occasional respite in our local children's hospice and, when his class at school was raising money for them, the teacher explained that it was a place for children who are dying. Michael was found crying in the playground later. I talked to him gently when he got home and explained that many people are working on a long-term treatment and a cure for HIV and each year there is new medication, which keeps him well. The life expectancy of people living with HIV increases every year and has changed so much since he came to me all those years ago. Michael has so much courage and determination that I think he stands a very good chance of reaching adulthood, and who knows then . . .

I believe caring for Michael has been a blessing for me and I have never regretted my decision to share our home with him. Although we have experienced great difficulties, we have faced them together as a family and our family unit has grown stronger in the face of adversity. Children like Michael are absolutely lovely. He is a beautiful young man and I am very proud of the wonderful young person he has become. Michael is just a young lad who wants to be accepted as normal.

| **Michael's view:**

My mum Debra is very skilled and is a good carer. She's somebody who doesn't mind what kinds of problems people have. She's good with foster children who come to stay with us. She's patient and caring. She doesn't shout. I think she's very good at making children feel confident. I feel safe living here because I know she loves me.

I think there should be more people like my mum who foster, because she's kind, caring and optimistic – which means she's positive about things. She keeps you up when you're feeling down. She is very loyal and I know I can rely on her. I know she would do anything for me.

Julie and Jason: **The pain of not understanding**

Sometimes it is thought that looking after babies and young children is the "easier" side of fostering. But every age group brings its own challenges, and Julie Lester and her partner, Vernon Hunter, find that children's emotional issues caused by separation and loss can be complex and painful, especially if the child has additional factors to deal with. Their foster child, Jason, has mild autism.

Julie Lestor, who is white, and Vernon Hunter, who is black Jamaican, have been together for 23 years, and have two older birth children and an adopted son. The couple, from London, began fostering six years ago and have had a mixture of emergency, short and long-term placements.

Julie tells their story:

We saw Jason in *Be My Parent* and there was something about his eyes that did it. We thought, yes, we can look after him. He was four years old, and had delayed development and mild autism. He was mixed heritage, white English and black Jamaican. He needed a long-term foster family because his mum is mentally ill. When she's well she's one of the best mums you can meet, but when she's ill she just lies in bed. His dad also has schizophrenia.

Jason had been with a foster carer who was in her 60s with no kids of her own. She was white and Jason was "white" because he'd always been with white people. I'm sure his carer loved him but he had no confidence because he never went anywhere. They watched telly at home all the time. He didn't know how to interact with other children, and the autism didn't help. The first time I took him to school, he ran up to a little boy and said 'Don't talk to me', and the other child ran off. My social worker thought it did him a world of good to be "thrown into the deep end" by coming into a busy family like ours and being taken to school.

The introduction to our family went well. Jason was pleased to come here and meet our children. But the first night he stayed, it dawned on him he that he was no longer with his other carer. He cried and cried, saying 'I want Trish and I want my mum'. It was heartbreaking. He was very scared. It was hard to know how much sense he could make of what was happening, and the change of routines must have been very difficult for him. I don't know much about autism, but I know about feelings. You could feel his pain. There's nothing you can do to take the pain away. So I sat with him and tried to reassure him: 'This is your new home but you are still going to see Trish and your mummy. If you sleep now, tomorrow we can go to the park and have one of those nice ice creams, and we can go for a drive, or to McDonald's.' I know it sounds like bribery but it helped him to sleep through the first few weeks. I just took it one day at a time.

He'd say, 'You are rubbish, this house is rubbish'. He completely rejected us. He'd refuse to do anything we asked. The first two weeks weren't so bad but then he really started to push the boundaries. He was screaming and throwing himself on the floor. He also started spitting, swearing and kicking furniture. He'd say 'I'm leaving, I'm going back to Trish! You have to take me!' I'd say gently but firmly, 'If you want to go you must go, but I'm not taking you.' I enlisted the help of his social worker who had known him for a long time. She explained to him that this was his new home, and it started to sink in a little.

He'd been quite spoilt. His mum had never been too hot on discipline and I think his previous carer had tried to compensate for his pain at leaving his mum. With his behaviour, it was hard to differentiate between his feelings, his autism and his age! We just had to reinforce the message that this was where he was going to live, and to explain that he would still be seeing Trish and his mummy. I was clear that behaviour like spitting and swearing wasn't acceptable. I didn't make a big issue of it, but he soon realised I wouldn't have that in my house. He stopped doing it at home but the behaviour started at school, and he was also smacking other kids. The school didn't know how to handle it and said things like, 'You can't go out and play with the boys if you behave like that'.

Jason's mind works totally differently from other children's minds. I've done courses on autism but I'm still only at the edge of understanding how he sees things. If you say something negative to Jason, the negative bits stick, so you have to focus on the positive. If I say to him, 'Try and be good at school today, don't be naughty,' he'd come home and say, 'You were right, I was naughty today'. It's better to say, 'I'm sure you're going to have a good day today, be good'. He'll come home and say, 'I was happy, I was good today'.

Sometimes you can divert Jason before he gets into a temper tantrum, with something like, 'Let's go and plant some seeds or maybe you'd like some chocolate?' But if he goes into a temper, he has to learn that it isn't going to wash with us. We'll say, 'OK, when you have finished throwing yourself on the floor and banging the furniture, you can come down and join us'. He's very strong-willed and he says he won't do this or that, but you have to be firm, consistent and show him the boundaries. He needs to understand the consequences of things he does. If he doesn't do his homework, then he doesn't get to watch *Mr Bean*. He'll say 'That's not fair', and we say, 'No, life isn't always fair but you are still going to do it', and then encourage him by praising his reading or whatever he's doing for homework. And afterwards he gets to watch his programme as a reward.

Some research says that children with autism don't like eye contact, but with Jason I find that the closer he is to me, and the more I hold the eye contact, the more it reinforces the messages for him. He likes to sit on my knee and have me touch him or hold his hand and that helps the information go in for him. He doesn't understand sarcasm at all but he's learning about jokes. He'll look at my eyes and see how I react, and he'll say, 'That's a joke, isn't it, Julie?' He's learning to interact. He finds it hard to communicate, but when you take him to school now he doesn't stand by us nervously. He'll go up to other children and say things like 'Do you like my hat?'

Jason is obsessive. He has a thing about cars and he's collected millions of them! And the button on the bus! Even if you are at the back, he has to press the button. And he says it over and over again, all the way: 'I press the button, I press the button.' Until he does it, your life isn't worth living! I haven't got a lot of patience but I've learnt to accept his behaviour. Once you recognise your weaknesses as well as your strengths, you learn to cope. I will still feel slightly irritated when he pushes past an older person to get to the button and they look at me like I'm an awful person who can't control my child, but I've learnt to smile and not get into arguments.

He has to have the same breakfast, the same dinner, the same drink before bed. I've accepted this because it's the only way to get Jason to eat. But I gauge his mood and, if I think I can get away with it, I'll introduce something new. Just a tiny piece, and it mustn't touch any of the other food, otherwise he won't eat at all. Slowly he will try the new food, especially if he sees the other kids eating it. His face looks like he's tasting medicine. Then over time he'll accept it and get addicted! You can't spring things on him, you have to take your time, hold him, look at him and explain everything very carefully.

When Jason came to us he thought he was white. We've tried to help him realise that if you have a black dad and a white mum you are mixed heritage. He might think he is white but other people see him as black, and it's important that children understand who they are. He'd compare his fair skin to mine and say, 'But I'm white like you', but we'd say, 'No, look at your hair and your nose. You are lucky, you have the best of both worlds, you are mixed heritage.'

It makes me sad when I see children who have lost their culture, and don't know about festivals, food and music from their heritage. We've introduced Jason to Jamaican food, and my husband Vernon and our children are really into music. Jason had very "sensible" clothes before and we've bought him things that are a bit trendier so he fits in at school. Vernon is really into sport and takes him to cricket, which is a very West Indian thing. We show him positive images of black people on the telly and famous people like Bob Marley. He now says he's "mixed race", and he has some understanding of how other people see him.

It's very hard for Jason that he can't live with his mother, but contact goes really well. His mum and I have a very good relationship and when he sees us talking and laughing, that's nice for him. When she goes home he is very sad, and he tells me that he misses her. I have to say: 'Yes, I know you do, but your mummy isn't well, and she's happy you are with us.' We phone his mum regularly and try to see his previous carer as much as we can, and he spends time with his aunt during school holidays. But sometimes it's hard to fit everyone in because there are only so many hours in a day!

I really feel for birth parents. One of the hardest things is collecting a baby from their mother at the hospital. When we go to pick up a baby I feel like dog dirt on someone's shoes because of what I'm doing to the parents. You know the child has to be paramount but it's a very sad time. I don't want mums to feel I'm physically wrenching their children from them, so I'll say something like, 'Why don't you dress her and put her on the chair, then you go out of the room and I'll just pick her up'.

I always try to think about how parents must feel if they are visiting their child in someone else's house. I ask them whether they want me to do the washing and feeding of the child, or whether they want to share it with me. Sometimes it's a struggle to remain professional if you feel you're building up a relationship with the parents and then discover they have so much resentment towards you. I worked with a birth mother who regularly came to our house for contact visits and shared so many of her problems with me. When it came to the court case, she made all sorts of complaints that the baby was dirty and I was feeding her the wrong things. It wasn't easy having contact with the mother after that because my instinct was to confront her about this, but I had to be professional and keep up a friendly, welcoming appearance.

The day a baby or child leaves is also another very sad time. It's something you never get used to. It is painful, a bit like the build-up to a funeral, but you can't let any of your feelings filter through to the child. If they're old enough you can prepare them for the experience, but with younger ones you just carry on loving and caring for them and hope the good attachment you've built up will help them attach to their new carers. If the child is going to a good place it does help, and you sometimes have the joy of the adopters to balance your feelings. But we've had one child go to relatives living in a really bleak house and that didn't feel so good. You have to be guided by professionals and accept the decisions they make. You're managing a whole whirlwind of feelings, but you remind yourself that you've done it before and you'll manage it again.

It's hard for us as adults but I can't imagine how hard it is for children to deal with all these painful things. I'd love to know how Jason's mind works, and what sense he makes of everything that's happened to him. He will tell you why he can't live with his mum or with his former carer, but I'm not sure what he actually understands by the words. But it's good to see him opening up, becoming happier, more receptive. He used to be a closed-up little boy with his head down. Now he's head-up, more confident, like a flower starting to blossom!

Philip and Roger: **Treating every young person as an individual**

One size doesn't fit all in fostering, and young people from similar backgrounds and circumstances may have very different needs. Whereas the first group of three Kosovan boys Philip Griffiths and Roger Taylor cared for turned out to be a complex but highly rewarding experience, the next four boys came with a personal agenda the couple found hard to meet. Only their commitment and enormous compassion towards young people helped them to weather the storm and not take it personally, when a young person rejected the help they were offering.

The couple, from the south of England, have fostered teenage boys for 13 years, and currently work for independent fostering providers. Initially they fostered jointly but, because of Roger's work commitments overseas, Philip is currently the main carer.

They have fostered more than 20 young people.

| **Philip tells their story:**

It was terrible to see the three lads when they first turned up. They were totally bewildered, quite scared, and the youngest, Besnik, started to cry. We'd had a call the day before to ask if we could take these three Kosovan young men who had just arrived in the country.

We'd been told they spoke no English, couldn't even say 'hello', and that very little was known about them. We'd never turned a placement down and these boys clearly needed somewhere to stay, so we said yes.

The youngest, Besnik, was 13, and his cousin, Dashamir, was 15. The oldest boy, Aleksander, was unrelated to the other two, and was also 15. You do tend to look at Kosovan young men and wonder if they are really the age they say they are, because they often look older. We have heard that they sometimes pass themselves off as younger in order to get help, but when you hear some of the things these boys have been through before coming here, you wonder if it's their experiences which have aged them. We didn't know the boys' stories until they were able to tell us themselves, but we later discovered that Aleksander's father had been killed by Serbs and he'd been separated from his mother while fleeing for safety. Besnik told us how one day Dashamir had just grabbed him and dragged him into a van, and how they'd travelled to England in that van. Besnik described the awful experience of everyone packed together for three days, suffering from diarrhoea and motion sickness. The boys had lost all contact with their families and we never knew who had arranged for them to come to England.

When social services brought the boys to us, there were no real plans for their future. Our role was to look after their immediate needs while they were assessed. We were given access to a language line which we could phone whenever we, or they, needed to explain something. Apart from that, all our early communications were through mime. We knew that the boys were non-practising Muslims and didn't eat pork, but we knew nothing else about their likes or dislikes. When you put food in front of them on the table, you worried about whether they were enjoying it or simply eating it because it had been given to them.

Those first few weeks were very difficult. We have quite a large house and the boys chose to stay in the back downstairs room, where there was a television. We would go through and watch videos with them, as a way of spending time with them. They barely came into the rest of the house apart from mealtimes, when we expected them to come and eat as part of the household. Then they'd scurry back into their room. We felt that was OK at that early stage. Everything was very strange for them and they needed the reassurance of being with each other. It did feel weird having these three strangers in our house, who we couldn't talk to and who we knew nothing about. All the usual things of showing young people around your home, finding out about them and what interests them, which you do when a child first moves in, just weren't possible.

Having the language line was useful for things like establishing bedtimes and some of the basic rules of the house. But it was also quite a performance getting through to someone who then had to find an Albanian speaker for you. I went into the back room one day and saw writing in blue pen all over the fabric of the couch. I phoned up the language line and explained, 'I have these three Kosovan young men in my house who have started doodling on my furniture, and I'd like to talk to them about why they've done this . . .' I knew it wasn't malice, they were obviously very bored and they'd also been badly affected by their experiences, but I felt I had to make it clear that some things weren't acceptable.

I remember we took them to a local market during those early days. They needed clothes and we wanted to help them make their allowance go as far as possible. They often asked to go back there and it was nice to know we'd taken them somewhere they'd enjoyed.

I think the turning point was when the boys started going to school. When it became clear that the lads were going to be a long-term placement, we started looking for schools. The boys were keen on this, they'd missed out on a lot of education at home because the Serbs had prevented Albanian children from attending school. So they'd often had lessons in the middle of the night or whenever someone could conduct a secret lesson. We used the language line to explain that we had arranged a meeting with the school, and that we would be taking them to buy their uniforms.

The school was brilliant. I explained that, as a gay couple, only one of us would turn up at parents' evenings because we know children can have a hard time from teasing. But the head of Besnik's year said that there were several same-sex couples who had children in the school. We found out several years later that she was lying to us, but with the very best intentions because she wanted us to feel comfortable! As a black woman she felt the school was too white and middle-class, and was very keen to have Kosovan children starting. She explained that the class Besnik was joining were a very nice, supportive group of children, which made us feel a lot better. The older boys' year wasn't going to be so easy, but they had each other so that wasn't quite so hard.

On their first morning Roger took the boys into the garden and photographed them in their school uniforms. They hadn't worn uniforms before and they were very smart and proud of themselves. We wanted to make it a special occasion for them. But it felt terrible taking them to school on that first day, and leaving them. I was near to tears! The designated teacher for children in care was wonderful and said I could go into the classroom with them if I wanted, but I felt that would make it twice as hard for them. I watched the two 15-year-olds going off looking a bit sheepish, but Besnik – who I was most worried about – went off happily and never looked back. The school had a buddy system so it meant that the boys had someone to take them around during that first week, and it helped to know they weren't on their own. I can't praise the school enough. They were always very good about things like providing interpreters for meetings, and it was the first school I'd come across where teachers actually turned up for young people's review meetings.

I collected the boys from school for the first few weeks. The boys clearly enjoyed going, especially Besnik who was in a lovely class. The big difference was that, having spent the day with new people, coming back to us was coming back to something familiar. We became much more important in the boys' lives, and from that time on the back room was hardly used. They started joining us in the

sitting room or the television room and becoming part of the family.
They started learning English at school, and at home we spent time
encouraging them in their reading. I remember we bought a book of
folk tales. We chose it because the stories were short and everything
was clearly illustrated with pictures, so even if they didn't
understand what they were reading they had some idea of what the
story was about. It was hard at times to remain patient as they spent
ten minutes struggling through the pronunciation of one word, but
you had to keep encouraging them! I remember one of the most
rewarding things – the first phone call they made to say 'Back at 11
o'clock'. It was so lovely to see them developing confidence and
independence.

I think we were even more important to them than to most of the
young people we foster, because they looked to us to explain
everything to them. English young people understand what a social
worker does and how the school system works, but these young
people knew nothing about that. We had to make every doctor,
dentist and optician appointment and accompany them to all of
them. We also went with them to all their meetings for their asylum
applications. Any letters they received they brought to us to read –
even after they'd moved out to live independently.

Alesksander and Dashamir moved to a training flat for independent
living when they were 17, and Besnik stayed with us until he was
18. Dashamir did an English course after leaving school and now
has a job, and Besnik – who's otherwise a very shy boy – decided
he wants a career in drama. Dashamir and Besnik have both
received permanent leave to remain in this country. At one point the
cousins were given 34 years' leave – which would have meant
they'd have had to leave when they were in their 50s, by which time
they'd probably have children and grandchildren! Fortunately that
was changed to permanent residence. But Aleksander had his
application turned down. We've never been able to understand why.
He has built his life here and he has no family to return to in
Kosovo. He is now married and wants to do something practical like

train to be a bricklayer or plumber – the sort of skills the country is crying out for! It's meant that he's never been able to relax and know his future is secure. At various times he and his wife have lived with us. He is supposed to have left the country but there's no way I could turn him away. We are the only family he knows.

I think it's very hard. We are encouraged to foster these young people, and when you're looking after young asylum seekers who are so dependent on you, it's likely that they are going to become part of your family and to keep ties with you after they leave care. But then the system wants to send them back – just because they are no longer children.

Besnik, Aleksander and Dashamir were excellent young men to care for. They wanted to take the opportunities on offer and we had no problems with them. We used to joke and say, 'If you want a quiet life as a foster carer, take young Albanians!' But every child is different and the later placements haven't been so straightforward. After Aleksander and Dashamir moved out, we were asked to take two other Kosovan boys: Edon, 14, and Viktor, 13. By now Besnik spoke good English and these boys had some English of their own. Edon was a delightful, cheeky young man and Viktor was very bright. We didn't know what their background was. By this time the war was coming to an end in Kosovo and they may have come to England in the hope of a better life. But what's wrong with that – doesn't everyone has a right to aspire to things? But I think they had expectations of living in London, and they'd spent their first months as part of an Albanian community in London. They found it hard that they were being moved outside London, where they'd be out of touch with their community.

These young people didn't want to be with us. You know it isn't personal. It isn't because they don't like you, or your home. It's just that they want to be somewhere else. At heart they were really nice kids. They came to us before Christmas and I wanted to make them feel very welcome. Christmas was always a magical time for me as a child and I wanted to make it special for them. Roger and I always spend far more than the allowance we are given for children's Christmas presents but we enjoy doing that. On Christmas night I'm always up until the early hours, putting together stockings and pillowcases for young people to open in the morning. Of course, with safe care you can't go into a young person's bedroom while they are asleep, so you have to leave everything downstairs – but it's still wonderful when they wake up and discover everything. That Christmas was hard work but the boys were amazed and thoroughly enjoyed it. I think they started to settle down after that.

It would probably have worked out well if we hadn't taken a third boy, Jetmir. This young man of 15 came to us with an obvious agenda. He very clearly didn't want to be here. He wanted to be in London. He was not an easy young person to trust and from the moment he arrived you could see him working on the two other boys. You do your very best for a child but it's very hard when they make it clear that they reject everything you are trying to give them. I've never ended a placement before, but after two months I mentioned to the social worker that I was considering asking for Jetmir to be moved. I could see that she thought I was exaggerating his behaviour, but after she had a meeting with him she came out saying, 'You can't put up with that! I'll move him.' It seemed that whatever she had tried to say to him about why he had to live with us and couldn't be in London, he'd cut her dead, interrupted her and refused to listen. It helped to know that my social worker recognised the problems we were facing, but it also makes me very sad when a placement ends like that.

We always insist before any young person comes to live with us that they are told that Roger and I are a gay couple. We feel it's important the young people know this, so there is no recrimination afterwards. But after Jetmir moved out, Edon and Viktor rang their social worker to say they couldn't stay in our house any longer because they'd just discovered Roger and I were gay. They claimed they knew nothing about this when they moved in. We knew – and their social worker knew – that this wasn't true. It was obvious that they saw this as a way of being moved back to London. There was a meeting with social services and at the meeting it was made clear that if the boys rejected our placement then social services wouldn't offer them anything else. I felt that wasn't right. I didn't want the boys to feel pressurised to stay with us if they didn't feel comfortable with us. So I told social services I would be ending the placement myself. That way I could make sure that social services would find them alternative carers.

It all happened so fast that the boys never returned to our house. A worker brought them round to collect their clothes when Roger and I were away. Our respite carers were staying at the time and, on the way out of the door, Edon turned to one of them and said, 'I have made a big mistake'. It was sad, they were very nice boys and they were young. You have to put it down to their age. Besnik was still living with us at this time and we realised that this might raise issues for him about living with a gay couple. We said, 'They have moved out, do you want to move?' but he said he was perfectly happy to stay with us.

Since Edon and Viktor, we've had another Kosovan lad called Ahmet. He was supposed to be 12 but we discovered he was actually 13. He's been one of the most challenging placements we've ever had but, like all the others, he's been through a lot. He came to us because we were told his previous foster carers couldn't manage him because he couldn't stick to rules. They could never persuade him to go to bed at night. We were told that his father had died when he was seven and, according to Kosovan culture, that made him the man of the house. From our experience of Kosovan culture, boys are very cosseted in the family. It seems that in most Kosovan families the women do all the household tasks and the men aren't expected to do anything. Kosovan males can be very dismissive of women, and male friends come before female relatives in the pecking order.

We've also been told by young people that there are definitely no gay people in Kosovo, and we've had to point out that there probably are, but they stay well hidden. We'll never forget being told by one young man, 'England is a very funny place: until I came to England I never saw a man with one leg before and I never saw two men living together!' You can't see their behaviour as homophobia or sexism because that's what they're used to. You just have to help them realise how things are here, and what is or isn't acceptable in our culture.

Ahmet had become separated from his mother and younger brothers. Somehow he'd got on a lorry and made his own way to Italy, where he'd been held for a while until he escaped. He was a very resourceful young man, who'd had to mature quickly to take responsibility as head of the household and then to look after himself. Maybe it's not surprising he finds it hard to return to being a "child" and having people impose boundaries on him. I suspect he's also got away with a lot because he's a very cute looking boy with a cheeky smile.

We had a houseful of Roger's work colleagues staying and they asked Ahmet, half-jokingly, if he was going on a trip to Wales with them. He said he was. I explained to him that he wasn't going because he had to go to school. He was adamant that he was going and I was adamant that he wasn't. He was very huffy about going to school the next day and that night he announced that he wasn't going to bed at his normal bedtime. He informed me that he was going to Besnik's room to watch television. There is very little you can do in those situations. You can't use physical force and it's a case of the young person's will against your own. So I decided to make my point in a different way. I took a calculated risk and locked the front door and the door to the downstairs television lounge. I then turned off the fuse for the upstairs rooms – but before doing so I called Besnik downstairs. Once Besnik was in the room with me I closed the door, leaving Ahmet stranded in the hallway with nothing to do. Ahmet sulked in the hallway for ten minutes but then I heard him going up to bed. He realised that I meant what I said when I told him I would not allow him to stay up.

Young people need to realise that I am the one in control in this
house. I'm someone who has to confront issues if there's a problem.
I'm not a person to fret about a problem and say nothing. As I've
got older, I've learnt to worry less and less about what young people
think of me, and to make it very clear when they are doing things I
don't find acceptable. That doesn't mean I don't care for them all
very much. Some nights I find myself going round knocking on
bedroom doors and calling out, 'I'm so glad you are here, I do love
you'. It's amazing how very tough-seeming Kosovan lads respond to
this. I get text messages from some of them ending with 'love' and
the boy's name. I suppose everyone likes to feel they are loved. It
helps to reassure them and enables them to settle and fit into the
family.

A lot of the things Ahmet does are because he can't understand why
things are the way they are. He couldn't understand why it's not
acceptable to miss school here when he'd probably only gone to
school a few days a week at home. With Ahmet I do a lot of talking
to try and explain things to him. It is tiring – it can be a constant
battle with Ahmet. Recently he was excluded from school for being
abusive to a teacher. He's also been truanting quite a lot. I explained
that being excluded didn't mean he could sit at home doing nothing
– he would be attending the pupil referral unit. But he refused to get
out of bed the next morning. There's nothing you can do. You can't
pull a quilt off a child and you certainly can't drag them out of bed.
I had to ring and say he wasn't coming in. At times like this you can
feel a failure, but you have to accept that as foster carers we don't
have all the answers. You can end up wondering if you've ever done
anything right, and what you could have done differently. You have
to try and remind yourself of the things you have achieved with the
particular young person, and with other children you've fostered.
You have to keep things in perspective.

Ahmet knows that if his behaviour continues to be so difficult we
may consider terminating the placement. It's not something I'd do
willingly but he's a boy who could achieve so much and at present

he's not getting much out of being here. I want him to think seriously about his future. I say to Ahmet, 'It's your behaviour I don't like, not you,' because no young person should feel they are being rejected.

Even when things are tough, I have no regrets about fostering. There's so much I'd have missed out on if I hadn't done this. Most of the young people stay in contact and for some of them, like Aleksander, we are their family. It gives me such a warm feeling when the phone goes and one of them says, 'Just a minute, I'll get my dad . . .'

5

Kathy and Francis:
Recognising strengths and limitations

Not every foster placement works out, and carers can find themselves coping with feelings of failure when a placement ends early. The pain of being unable to support a severely sexually abused child caused Kathy and Francis Towler to question their ability to foster. However, taking on two confused and angry little girls – who are now very much part of their lives – restored their confidence and helped them to realise that every family has to recognise its strengths and limitations, in order to foster successfully.

Kathy and Francis Towler, from northern England, have fostered for four years. They have a birth daughter and an adopted daughter. Kathy and Francis decided to foster as a way of using the skills they learnt from their preparation for adoption, and in order to "give something back" to their local authority. They now foster for an independent fostering provider.

I **Kathy tells their story:**

Natalie was the first child we fostered – and nearly the last! She came for respite but then it turned out that the foster carer didn't want her back, so we guessed she had problems. But we agreed to take her as a short-term placement, knowing very little about her. We'd been told she had global development delay, which means that, because the child has been neglected or the mother hasn't looked after herself during pregnancy, the child's development is slow. She was attending special school and had learnt sign language. She was eight years old.

We were told that Natalie was faecally incontinent but if we gave her laxatives once a week there would be no problems. She was wearing nappies which she found really degrading. And she smelt all the time which was bad for her self-confidence. But once she came to us it was obvious that there was a much bigger problem. She had a complete fear of the toilet. Trying to get her anywhere near it was a huge psychological barrier. She would peer anxiously through the door and flick her fingers, which she did when she was stressed. She'd say, 'It's going to flood'. I would take the cistern lid off so she could look inside and see it was alright. It was easier to get her to go for a wee in the shower. We also said you can use the toilet and keep the door open if you feel safer. I'd then stay upstairs but somewhere out of sight and my husband would make sure he was downstairs.

Nobody had really looked at why this child was so frightened of using the toilet. But we started to piece together the details. After a couple of months she disclosed to me the things she'd experienced – the abuse she'd suffered at the hands of her grandfather. She told me she had "pooed" on his face and he'd flushed her head down the toilet. Natalie would masturbate anywhere in the house because this man had told her that 'a shag makes you feel better'. She would try and sit on men's knees and stroke their jeans. It got to the stage where men who came to the house didn't dare sit down. My husband made cakes with her once. She got so excited about the attention that she started to masturbate. She wouldn't eat sausages or white sauce or vanilla yoghurt – she was gagging on these foods. You had to mix in food colouring to help her eat them. Yet she'd eat out of the dog bowl.

I don't think our own children were really aware of her behaviour, but we used to say 'No, Nat, if you want to do that, do it in private in your bedroom'. And you have to be very aware of safe care. We had a strict rule that my husband never went into her bedroom, and was never in any room with her alone. If it had to happen for some reason, then he ensured that the rest of us were around and the doors were open. She could so easily misconstrue things so you had to be so careful. I remember she was dozing off in front of the telly one day and my husband ruffled her hair gently in passing. The next day she told me, all gooey and flirty, that Francis had "tickled" her while she was asleep.

I remember the first time she disclosed I was with her in the playroom clearing up. She had her back to me. She said, 'Why did my granddad put his willy on my face?' I just picked up a piece of paper and a crayon and started writing it all down. I tried to pretend I was still packing away and made sure I stayed calm. She told me some details about the abuse. Then she asked, 'What's for tea tonight?' Her conversations were always like that – she'd jump from one subject to another.

After this conversation I was shaking. I phoned her social worker and said, 'what shall I say to her?' I felt we'd skimmed over disclosure in the preparation and I wanted someone to come and talk to me about how to respond appropriately to her. But it was a couple of days before anyone came to see me. I had to attend child protection interviews with Natalie. Once the floodgates opened she would tell you anything, anywhere – even in the queue in Tesco. We had to tell her that she could only say this when she was with the child protection officer.

From this contact with the police I started to put together snippets of information. We discovered that Natalie came from a large family where all the younger children had been sexually abused. It seemed that the children had been "bred" for a paedophile ring – which involved the parents and grandparents. The family were well known to the police and one member was a Schedule 1 offender*. I

* "Schedule 1 offender" is a term used to refer to people who have been convicted of an offence listed in Schedule 1 to the Children and Young Persons Act 1933 – largely offences against children, for example, cruelty or violence.

discovered that they lived fairly near us. Natalie had been in foster care for two years but nobody had thought to get her any professional help. I kept saying to the social workers, this child needs therapy. They agreed in principle, but apparently there was a five month waiting list.

Because Natalie was a child with special needs, the police decided not to proceed with the prosecution. The police knew that the granddad had abused the children and that he had targeted the "special needs" children who couldn't stand up to give evidence against him in court. It was the most frustrating thing. I was in pieces – Natalie was still telling me things and they were going round in my head. I'd think, suppose I'm out shopping and this man who abused her comes towards me. She loved this man because he'd showed her affection. She didn't know the difference. But I didn't know how I'd stop myself from screaming at him for what he'd done to her. I had to stop shopping in town during this period.

In the end it got too much for us and we had to ask for her to be moved. She'd only been with us about four months. We weren't really prepared for something so complicated for our first foster placement. We gave eight weeks' notice and I was tearful all through that time. I got to the stage where I dreaded Natalie coming home from school and asking questions I couldn't give her answers to. I felt guilty and angry and I couldn't sleep. It began to affect my relationship with Francis. When you hear things like this from a child, you can get to the stage where you don't want a man anywhere near you. The child protection officer was the only person who really helped me, by putting me in touch with a counsellor. They helped me to realise that everyone finds it hard to listen to such distressing things, but it's even harder when the person you're hearing it from is living under your roof and you can't get away from it.

Natalie had no concept of time so I had to tell her just before she was due to leave us. And I bought her a teddy bear hot water bottle to take with her. We'd also taught her to say 'I'm a happy, friendly, pretty little girl' because her abuser had told her she was a 'whore and a bitch'. So we made a game of it where we'd ask her to describe herself and we'd say 'What are you, Nat?' and she'd say 'A happy, friendly, pretty little girl'. We had those words printed and laminated and I put them together with the hot water bottle. I remember tearing myself up inside when the new foster carer came to take her away.

I've kept in touch with her foster carer and I still send Nat birthday and Christmas cards. It helped with my feelings of guilt to know that I could tell her new carer some of the things we'd found helpful with Nat, so she didn't have to start all over again. Her carer tells me that she's now having therapy but she's still faecally incontinent and she still behaves inappropriately with men. Her carer is at her wits' end to know how to help her. I think, looking back, there's so much emphasis on giving these children a family life – which professionals think has to be a mum, dad, brothers and sisters. But I wonder if, for some children, it could equally be three or four workers in a specialist unit who really care for them, and can give them immediate access to the therapeutic help they need, at least for an initial period.

At the time we felt such failures. But it really was too much for us in our first foster placement. The workers should have told us she had such complex needs. After fostering Natalie, we had to stop fostering for six months. Then we started to think there must be an agency out there that does fostering right. We looked around and we "interviewed" three independent fostering agencies about the level of support they offered. We found an agency where our worker visits us regularly and we receive the type of support we need.

Opal and Pearl were the first children our new agency placed with us. Opal was nine and Pearl was seven. We were intended as a "bridge" placement before they moved on to another more permanent placement. They'd come straight from an adoptive placement that had broken down after three years. It seemed the adopter had never wanted two children. In their short life they'd had

15 different moves – some with birth family relatives, some with their mum and her various partners, some with their birth dad, as well as three moves to the same foster carer.

The children had witnessed and experienced a lot of domestic violence when they were younger. Opal told me very calmly how they'd both been hiding under the bed while their mother's partner was brandishing a knife and threatening to harm them. He'd then pulled Pearl out and taken her downstairs and broken and slashed her arm. Pearl was about three-and-a-half at the time, and Opal was five. When the police were called, they found the children dirty, unkempt and malnourished.

Pearl was very upset about the failed adoption – her adopter kept in contact for a short time before they left the country a couple of weeks later. Opal had found it hard because the adopter seemed to have favoured the younger child. She told me, 'I knew she didn't want me,' and she'd clearly been left out of many things. Both girls had huge attachment issues – they didn't want to trust anyone.

When they arrived, they behaved like perfect little girls who were desperate to please. You just knew they couldn't be that perfect, and it soon started to wear off. Opal was trying very hard to be good and every so often it would slip. The pressure became too much, and she would kick and punch me. A lot of the anger was aimed at me because her birth mother left her without saying goodbye. She would swear at me and call me everything under the sun. She would swipe everything off a surface in her anger. In the first year, she saw us as able to provide her with food and shelter but no security. And that was what she craved the most. One minute she'd be fine, helping you get tea ready and you'd be saying something about how she was doing well at school. And she'd say, 'I'm not going to be here next year, so why should I be good at school?' Her behaviour would then spiral out of control and one of the younger children we were fostering would get a kick. We had to anticipate the behaviour and get the younger children safely into another room. We've been on lots of courses to learn to manage Opal's behaviour and these days her tantrums are far less frequent, and last only a fraction of the time.

Opal was a very mixed-up little girl. She remembers all of the pain of her early years, whereas Pearl lives in a fantasy land. When Pearl first came, she just smiled all the time. Opal knows she's putting on a mask but I don't think Pearl knows that she's doing this. I think she learnt early on to be a very closed book for her own protection. She is very matter-of-fact about her arm being broken. When the name of the man crops up, she will say that that was the name of the man who cut her. I'm sure her feelings will come out later on, and we are prepared to get her the support she may need. But at the moment she comes across as a happy little girl who jokes but can't remember anything practical. At school they tell me she still goes into the wrong maths or English group. I have everything written down to help her remember. I feel that, as long as she can learn some useful life skill like how to use money, she should be all right. She's never going to be a brain surgeon but she's steaming ahead with her swimming lessons. I try and make sure they all have chances to do things where they can succeed and raise their self-esteem.

Opal clearly has a lot of anger and confusion inside which shows itself clearly in her behaviour. When Opal kicked me I'd say, 'How do you think I feel? I feel really upset and angry because you kicked me and I'm going into the other room now to calm down.' We try to talk to them all the time about feelings and how they affect you. These children so often bottle things up that it comes out in anger, so we try to give them the words to talk about their emotions.

It's important for Pearl to learn how to show her emotions. I try to help her pinpoint her feelings. She's a vulnerable child and it's important that she knows if a situation is unsafe. I say to her, 'You can't be polite all the time Pearl, sometimes if you feel scared you just have to run away'. It's great when she comes home from school and tells me that she felt sick in her tummy when this thing happened at school – it shows she's beginning to recognise her feelings and listen to them.

Opal would "squirrel" things away. She'd bring other people's pens and rubbers home from school, and she'd take things from my eldest daughter's bedroom. She even took an exercise book and copied out a play which my eldest daughter had written. She so badly wanted to belong to our family that it was as if she was trying to become her.

To begin with, I used to go into her room while she was at school and put back everything she'd taken from other people's bedrooms. But the other girls do get fed up with her taking things. You can lift up the mattress and find one of the other girls' earrings and she'll still say she hasn't taken them. You can't really tell when she's lying so it's frustrating to deal with. So we have certain rules to try to prevent things getting out of hand. We introduced a rule around "swopping", which all has to go through me, so that it's very clear whether something is being lent, given, or has been taken without permission. We also have an "amnesty" box on the landing so that, if you find anything that isn't yours when you are tidying your bedroom, you just put it in the box. That way you don't get into arguments and blame. That worked well for a while and soon we didn't need it any more. But you have to be prepared to try something different when one method stops working.

The girls both had very low self-esteem and we always try and give children as many opportunities as possible to try out things and find out what they enjoy and are good at. Opal does quite well at school but she goes around looking like a thundercloud. I say to her, it's your choice about what you do with your life. People give you opportunities but only you decide how to use them. You've had a difficult life but people won't make allowances for that when it comes to applying for a job. So you have to decide whether you want to become the kind of person people want to have around.

It's important to try to help children understand that actions have consequences. When they've been pushed around by adults and lied to for much of their lives, you can't expect them to believe what you are saying. They need opportunities to realise things for themselves. I will advise Opal not to go around in bare feet, but I can't force her to wear shoes. Her bedroom's a tip and the other day she stood on a make-up mirror and cut her foot. As a result she couldn't take part in sports day or go skating. We went camping last year and she was adamant that she didn't need sunscreen, even though we explained that sunburn is really painful. And she will insist on wearing boots without socks even though you know she's going to get horrible blisters. It can be hard to stand back and let a child make these mistakes but, as our link worker says, we are here to guide them not to dictate to them, and if they're not in any form of serious danger then it's a good learning opportunity. I think you need to pick your battles carefully. If the child isn't at serious risk, it probably isn't worth a major confrontation, and it's better to let them discover the consequences of their actions for themselves.

My two older daughters tell me that other parents ground their children for weeks or threaten to stop several months' pocket money, but I don't believe in these sorts of excessive punishments. You need to choose something that is meaningful to the child which you can keep to, and which is time-limited. We have a whiteboard in the living room. If someone doesn't do their household chores – which are always age-appropriate – then I write up that they've lost a pound from their pocket money. They'll be desperate to win it back, and you find ways to let them do this.

After about nine months, we started to get a chink of the real Opal coming through. The temper tantrums became less frequent and less intense, and she'd be able to apologise. Or admit she'd done something, which was always very hard for her to do. I introduced a notebook beside her bed so that she can write messages for me. Or she'll say she's sorry and I'll give her a hug and remind her that that kind of behaviour is not on! But it was also a difficult time for her. The girls' granddad died suddenly and he'd been the one strong male in Opal's life. She's never had a dad, whereas Pearl has some contact with her dad – albeit quite difficult at times. Opal was also worrying a lot about her birth mother who had disappeared. The loss of her grandfather was another sudden ending, where she'd not had a chance to say goodbye. We starting getting some regular help from CAMHS*, which has been helpful.

Around this time social services started looking for a permanent foster placement for the girls. We were only meant to be a bridging placement. I said we'd like to be considered, but they felt it wouldn't work because Pearl and Opal were too close in age to our own girls. They showed us research which shows that most breakdowns in placements are where children in the family household are too close in age. But I did my own research – reading things like BAAF's book *Growing up in Foster Care* (see Useful Resources) – and what I found was that the real key to breakdowns was that carers tend to treat children of the same age in the same way. We've always been so conscious of the importance of treating every child as an individual. So if one goes to Brownies, the other is going to dance class. If one child has friends around, then we keep the other children separate, so they don't poach each other's friends and each child has something for themselves.

Fortunately, it was recognised that, if the girls moved again and it didn't work out, this could have a very damaging effect. The girls had therapy which was used to assess their relationship to their birth family and to us. The girls were always writing us letters saying please can we stay with you. It's so tempting to say yes, of course you can, but it's awful to give a child false hope. What we did give them very clearly was the message that we loved them very much and would always care about them. We tried to hide it from the girls until we knew for sure what was happening, but we had to tell them in the end because the social worker was coming to our house to assess us.

When the full Care Order was granted, the agency gave the children

* the Child and Adolescent Mental Health Services.

money to take us out for a meal. They chose a restaurant for us to go to. We made that a Family Day which we celebrate every year.

Around that time, Opal's behaviour went off the wall. The girls were snipping at each other constantly and Opal was always pinching or swearing at her sister. Opal threatened to commit suicide and was self-harming, cutting her wrists with plastic, picking her nails until they bled, refusing to drink anything and flying into temper tantrums. There'd been so much going on with visits from social workers and court dates, and then suddenly it all tailed off. When the decision that we could foster them long-term came through, it was like – is that it? Is this all? They'd got the security they craved and there was a short spell of euphoria, after which a bit of an anti-climax set in. Fortunately we'd had training about dealing with tantrums before they escalate. Opal explained that, when she starts to get violent, she can't stop. So my husband came up with a code word. He told her that when she got into a mood he would say 'elephants', so it was a signal to her that she needed to be by herself. The first time she stopped and walked off instead of just erupting on the spot, we knew she was making progress. At her therapy sessions they gave her a certificate which said 'Opal, the world's greatest elephant trainer'. She now has a real sense of achievement because she's learning to take herself off when it gets too much. And she only blows up once every few months.

I also find that it really helps to use relaxation techniques to calm children down when they are distressed. I've been on training courses to learn about Indian head massage and I use lavender oils and relaxing music. Opal has a hand massage every night, even when she's been violent. It's a way of touching a child which isn't threatening. When she's in a mood, she feels that no one can love her, so I ask her to go and get the hand cream and she starts to relax straight away. When a child is in a mood you can't really say, 'Come and give me a hug', because they won't be receptive, but with the massage we end on a positive note and she can go to bed having had that close contact.

Nothing seems to faze Pearl, and you barely notice her tantrums.
But I'm sure her feelings will come out when she's older, maybe
when she's a teenager. We see ourselves as a base for the children as
they grow into adults. We have never said that we can guarantee to
keep them for the next ten years, but we will have them for as long
as we can manage them. There are some behaviours we wouldn't be
able to put up with, like a child drawing a knife on us or other
children. But in the same way, we wouldn't throw them out at 18.
They may choose to seek independence at 16, at 20, or at 30. We
have a studio flat attached to my husband's business, so we can help
them put their foot into the water towards independence while still
being there for them.

The girls will always be welcome as much as our other children.
And it's important for them to feel that our home is somewhere
where they can have a sense of history, somewhere where they can
talk about what their birth mum was like the last time she saw them.
I keep a daily diary for each child and I've written down things that
have happened while they've been with us. Like when we went to
Center Parcs and they had plum tomato soup and Pearl said, 'I like
tomato soup, but not plums'. Little things which are so important in
giving them a sense of security, and a past that is rooted somewhere.

Francis's view:

I think fostering works for the two of us, because we have a sense of
humour and we're a good partnership. Kathy and I describe
ourselves as a "tag team". When one of us is getting tired or
emotional, then the other one takes over. We talk to each other about
what we have said to the children, or what decisions we've made, so
that we give them consistency. That way, children can't play us off
against one another!

It's not what children do to you – it's what you do to yourself that
you need to keep a check on. You have to learn to put your feelings
behind you. If you start beating yourself up, feeling guilt or anger
about their behaviour, then you have lost the battle. As the foster

carer, you must be the strong one. You have to give children the flexibility to make choices, even if it saddens you when they don't make the choices you'd like them to make.

If you expect nothing back from the children you foster, then anything they give you is a bonus. If you let your expectations start to go up because things have gone well for a couple of months, then you can get hurt when things go wrong again. You need to see the good times as a bonus, but don't expect the child to be able to change in the way you'd like them to. You can never make up to a child the bad experiences they've been through in the past, but you can give them the confidence to make their own choices and live with them. You can help them realise that they don't have to take a certain route just because they've been in care.

6

Jabeen and Hussain: **Helping a severely disabled child to live in the community**

Caring for a severely disabled child is a huge challenge but Jabeen and Hussain Qadri and their children chose this particular type of fostering. Despite having no previous experience of caring for children with disabilities, they have helped to change Jamaal, a withdrawn, aggressive boy with learning disabilities, into a happy, outgoing child who is very much part of their family.

Jabeen and Hussain, an Asian Muslim couple from the North of England, have three birth children of their own. They foster through a Barnardo's specialist scheme for children with disabilities. Jamaal is a long-term placement and has been with them for two-and-a-half years.

Jabeen tells their story:

My own children were growing up and everyone told me how well they were doing. My oldest daughter was married and we had a spare bedroom, and I thought, 'Why don't we open our home to a child with special needs?' My sister fosters and I'd stayed with her when I first came to England, so I knew something about it. I talked to my husband and my children. But it was my son who said to me, 'Everyone wants able-bodied children – why don't we have a disabled child?' He'd been to a nursery with a disabled child and it had stuck in his mind as he grew up.

I saw that Barnardo's was looking for carers for disabled children. I hadn't met any disabled children before but I felt that this was something I could do. Barnardo's was really fast to respond. There was very good training on children with special needs. We were then assessed and approved. We were told we would meet children and we didn't have to agree to take the first child we met. But Jamaal was the first child we met. I had it in my mind that Allah wants us to take this child, it is our destiny to have this child.

Only my husband and I went to visit him first at the children's home. Jamaal was very introverted, there was no eye contact. He turned his head from side to side. He was 11 years old, from an Asian Muslim background. He was hearing impaired and did not speak. He had been affected by rubella and had a severe learning disability and behaviour problems. I was told that he functioned around the age of a two-year-old child. He was living in a children's home because his family could no longer cope with his behaviour.

I felt I could have Jamaal to live with us, so he came to visit us with his social worker. I saw the problems from the start. The first time he was in our house he took his pad off and wet the carpet. He was a very strong-willed child and the social worker, my husband and I, between us, couldn't persuade him to put the pad back on. I have noticed that children with special needs, even if they look very frail, can have so much strength. Obviously you are not allowed to use force, and he was very stubborn.

There was one visit a week to our house for four months, so we could get to know Jamaal and learn about his care. Then he came to stay for a night, and after that he moved in. It was hard work, it was a challenge, but my family supported me. He would wake up at two or three o'clock in the morning and start giggling. I couldn't leave him because he couldn't express his needs, so I had to stay with him until he went back to sleep. It was a long time before Jamaal felt secure enough to sleep through the night, but now he's been with us for more than two years and he sleeps well.

I couldn't leave Jamaal alone with my boys because of his behaviour. Jamaal didn't know how to share and he was used to watching television all day. I think in the residential home they were very busy with the other children whose needs were more complicated than Jamaal's. When one of my boys tried to change the television channel, Jamaal head-butted him. At first my boys were afraid to be in the room with him and stayed up in their bedrooms. But my husband told the boys to come downstairs and that he would be there. When Jamaal tried to head-butt them, my husband switched off the television. We had to teach Jamaal to share. If he misbehaved when someone wanted to watch another programme, we would take him away from the television. I would have him with me in the kitchen. Jamaal is a child who needs very clear boundaries. When he would slap and head-butt my boys, and they came to me, I said to them, 'Don't hit back. Just hold his hands and say firmly: "Don't do that to me"'.

Jamaal had received very little stimulation. He had hearing aids but no one had encouraged him to use them. We learnt some signs like "toilet" so we could communicate with him. He used the PECS system – it has photographs of the different things a child might need. If you want to ask him if he wants a drink, you give him the card with the drink symbol on it. Or he can give you the card with the toilet symbol on it. But when he first came, he didn't want to use the cards and he pushed them away. He wanted to be like the other children. So I mime things to him, but I also speak and he has learnt to read my lips. I noticed that he watched programmes like *Home and Away* on television and he seemed to understand the English. He understands Urdu as well. He also loves the news on television, he won't miss it! If he sees war scenes and someone being taken to hospital, he has a good laugh. He had been in hospital a lot as a young child and maybe it helps him to feel that he isn't the only one!

We're trying to toilet-train him and we're following a programme. He knows the "thumbs up" signal – the sign language for OK – and he puts his thumb up to ask me if he has been a good boy. He's making good progress. He now comes and shows me the PECS sign when he needs to go to the toilet. We've got to the stage where he has only one pad a day. During the review meetings I explain to the school what I'm doing and ask them to do the same. I have a very good social worker who supports me.

When Jamaal arrived he didn't know how to swallow solid food. He was on a nutritious drink. Maybe it was because of medical problems from the past, but he seemed to have a "phobia" about solid food. We enjoy our meals together as a family and we wanted him to be a part of that. I started him with baby food, and he seemed to like that. I gave him fromage frais and yoghurts with bits of fruit in it. He is now able to eat the same food as we do, but I have to puree it first. I think that one day he'll be able to eat solid food.

He used to spill drink or soup on himself. I would rush him to the shower. He loves water, he'd be giggling and smiling while I showered him. I talked this through with the educational psychologist and she suggested some different approaches. So one day when he deliberately spilt a drink on himself, I made him sit in the dining room for a little while, and I explained that I wasn't giving him a shower until later on. He is a very particular child and he hates being sticky. He realised that this wasn't the way to get a shower and he doesn't tip things over himself now.

You have to find out about the child and what they like and don't like. Then you can reward them but also take things away to show them that you don't like their behaviour. Jamaal has a "twiddler", a very small toy he holds in his hands all the time. When he first arrived, he threw a pot plant and he pushed the television and broke it. When his behaviour is difficult we take his "twiddler" away from him, or we take him away from the television. My social worker recommended doing this for 10 minutes but with Jamaal it needs to be longer so he understands. Each child is different and you have to find out what helps them to learn. You need to take it very slowly and reinforce messages, over and over again.

Jamaal learns from the other children's behaviour. He's learning about emotions. Before, his feelings came out through aggressive behaviour – he would throw himself down in anger. He doesn't do this now at home, although he sometimes does it at school. He sees that my children don't slap and head-butt people when they are angry. He didn't cry when he first came to us, but now his eyes fill up with tears when he is upset. He's learnt it's better to cry than to hurt other people. He understands things like love. When my children come to me for a hug, he will push them away because he wants the first hug.

Taking Jamaal into the community used to be a big problem. Just trying to get to the car was difficult, he would throw himself down. When we went to town he started grabbing people. He would hold on really tight. People were usually very understanding because he has special needs, but he started doing it a lot and we knew we had to stop this behaviour. When he grabbed someone, I would stop what we were doing and take him home. He thought that was a quick way to get home to watch TV, but he learnt that we wouldn't let him watch TV when he had misbehaved. When he said he was sorry we would take him out again for a few minutes. If he misbehaved, we would repeat the pattern and come home again, or I would make him sit in the car with me or my daughter, which he didn't like. Sometimes everyone would go out and leave him behind with my husband or myself. Those who were going out would show him how happy they were to be going out and we would tell him – through miming pulling at our clothes – that they were leaving him behind because we didn't like the way he grabbed people.

Over a year we started seeing changes in his behaviour. Now he can be very well behaved. We can take him to the doctor's surgery and he will get into the car without a fuss, and let the doctor look at him. We've started taking him to restaurants and cinemas. He loves to go shopping and choose his clothes. Before, when I took him shopping, he was very introverted, but now if you show him clothes he knows what he likes and he enjoys picking things. He's mad about brand labels; my boys are only just taking an interest but Jamaal has liked Reebok clothes since he arrived. He would try and pull a Reebok t-shirt off someone's back! He loves Thomas the Tank Engine and Harry Potter and he wanted Harry Potter pyjamas.

Sometimes when we are out, Jamaal still pretends to grab. You see a cheeky smile on his face as he puts his hand out. We say, 'Do you want to go home?' and he stops. He knows it's not the thing to do and he doesn't do it. He is aware that he is achieving things. I don't think he had very much praise before, and his self-confidence has really developed.

Jamaal doesn't like going to school and getting him ready to go is never easy. He is collected every day by an escort in a taxi. But he loves coming home from school. At first I would meet him at the door and take his coat and shoes off. Now he takes his own jacket and shoes off and he comes into the kitchen to see if tea is ready. If I'm busy, I can tell him to go and play in the conservatory until the meal is prepared. There was a time when there would have been a big fuss if I asked him to do this, but now he does what I ask.

Jamaal also now plays board games with my sons – he throws the dice and the boys move the counters for him. He has a go on the GameBoy when the boys play. When it's homework time, I give him some paper and a pen and he scribbles, or plays with his puzzle while the boys work. He has quite an advanced puzzle. He sees that my children love football and the boys have taught him to kick. They also throw balls for him to catch. Once he mixed up five jigsaws together and I asked him to separate the pieces. He was able to do that, so we know he can differentiate between different colours. He is also learning to form some of the letters of the alphabet.

Jamaal has contact with his family twice a year. Some foster carers have really good relationships with their foster child's birth parents,

but I think it is difficult for birth parents when they see their child
doing well with someone else. They can see Jamaal is a changed
boy and they probably feel they have failed and wonder why
couldn't they do the things we have done. I'm sure it is difficult for
them and I don't blame them for not feeling comfortable with us. I
think maybe I was just lucky to have these skills to look after a
disabled child, and the training from Barnardo's enhanced them.

For the first two years that Jamaal was with us, we didn't visit our
families in our home countries. We felt it was important for Jamaal
to have stability. When we did go to see my parents, Jamaal went to
short-term break (previously called respite) care. I wrote everything
down for the carers, and Jamaal had gradual introductions to them.
When we came back, my sons were so keen to see Jamaal again,
they had really missed him! It's good to have the short-term break
carers so we can have 24-hour breaks or breaks in case someone is
ill. We have taken Jamaal on holiday in Europe and to south Wales.
He enjoyed his holidays and everyone was surprised that we
managed to cope with taking him.

We are practising Muslims and we wanted to foster a Muslim child.
We don't feel it would be fair to force a child from a different
religion to pray with us or follow our customs. Jamaal goes to the
mosque with my children. Children with special needs are very
welcome in Muslim communities. In our religion, if a child has
special needs there is perhaps a tendency to spoil them too much.
Sometimes friends try to be kind and say it doesn't matter if Jamaal
does this or that in their house, because they don't understand how
important it is for Jamaal to have firm boundaries. When we visit
friends, my husband and I stay in a hotel with Jamaal, and our
other children stay in the friends' house, so we can keep Jamaal's
routines. But our friends are so supportive, everyone takes an
interest in Jamaal. When people send us cards or presents they
always include Jamaal with the other children. I love it when my
family and friends tell me how much Jamaal is improving, that he's
a different child.

Looking after Jamaal is hard work but it's rewarding – I don't regret doing this. When I go to bed at night I'm a satisfied person. The most important thing for a child is security and love. Jamaal has those things here. He has grown and put on weight, and his social worker describes him as a happy child.

Robin and Louise:
A serious case of neglect

One of the hardest things about fostering is knowing that sometimes you may have little or no say about the fate of children you are caring for. Robin and Louise Beswick still find it hard to believe that four siblings, who had flourished in their family after experiencing the worse neglect the couple had ever come across, were eventually returned to the parent who had failed to care for them.

Louise was fostering when Robin first met her, and he gave up his job in the city to train as a foster carer. The couple, who are white and from the west of England, bought a large house together so they could take sibling groups, and are employed by an independent fostering provider. Louise has four birth children from her first marriage and Robin has two. Two of Louise's children currently live with the family.

Robin tells their story:

We got a phone call at around three o'clock from the duty social worker at our agency who asked us to take a sibling group of three from one of the London boroughs. It was to be a boy of 12, his eight-year-old brother and their sister who was four. Then there was another call at about 5pm to say that, on entering the premises, the police had found a 12-month-old baby that no one had been aware of. This child had never been registered. We said we had the room, not a problem. We'd taken large numbers of children in the past so we pretty well knew what to expect. But these children were in the most horrific state, like something you might find in a Dickens novel!

The children arrived with two social workers and a police officer. The two younger ones were wrapped in blankets, the two older children were quite literally in rags. All the children were malnourished, some of them mere skin and bones, and they were all filthy. The dirt was ingrained. Their hair was lank and greasy, and you could see the lice moving on their heads. The pallor of their skin was something we hadn't come across before – it was almost fluorescent from lack of daylight.

The children were found because a Jehovah's Witness, who had knocked on their door, heard a baby crying and looked through the letterbox, and was almost physically sick at what she saw. She called the NSPCC, who alerted social services. There was no furniture in the house. No electricity or water. Downstairs was uninhabitable so they were living upstairs. A social worker who had seen it described it to us as looking like a 'dirty protest'. The house was condemned and then gutted after the children were removed. The children's mum had a major drug problem and was regularly in hospital. She would just leave the kids to get on with it. When she was around, the mother was working as a prostitute and probably bringing clients back. The older children had recurring nightmares about people standing over their beds and the house burning down. The family had been known to social services for some time, but nobody had provided the support that was needed. It seemed to us that there had been a colossal failure of agencies for things to have reached this stage.

Paul, the 12-year-old, was the carer for the other three children. When he arrived he wouldn't let go of the baby. He'd missed an entire year of secondary school by staying at home to look after the others. The baby had never had baby milk, only chips and milk from bottles which Paul had stolen from doorsteps and supermarkets. And from the minute Nicola, the four-year-old girl, walked through the door, she clung to Louise. I think she just needed the reassurance of someone female. And Ewan, the eight-year-old, was a jack-in-the-box, "hyper" from the moment he arrived.

After we went through the documentation with the social workers, we got all of the children into baths. We started with Kyle, the baby, who had a severe ear infection and was in a lot of pain. We had a sleepless night as he cried non-stop. It was also very unsettling for Paul. We'd had to prise Kyle out of his arms, and he wasn't happy with us having the baby in our room while he slept in his own bedroom.

The two older boys bathed themselves and I took clothes up to them. We keep drawers full of jogging bottoms and tops for a wide age range, so we always have something kids can change into. I took the clothes in as an opportunity to have a quick glance over their bodies for injuries or signs of abuse. Louise had done the same thing with Nicola – and had spotted cigarette burns on her body. At times like this, and particularly as a male carer, you always have to be aware of safe care. I'd always knock on the door if children were in the bathroom or bedroom and allow them to come out and talk to me, rather than going in. I would never go into girls' bedrooms unless they are fully clothed, and then I'd stay within the doorway. So when checking on the boys in the bathroom, I waited until they were partially dressed, kept at least an arm's distance away from them and left the door wide open. You need to find out what an individual child feels comfortable with – if you feel that they are not comfortable, you take a couple of steps back and give them more space.

The following morning I went shopping and filled the car boot with four huge bags of clothes for the children, clothes that they could call their own. They were extremely happy about getting their own clothes. From the first day, Louise started to work on Nicola's self-esteem. This little girl was very withdrawn, and constantly said that she was ugly and that nobody liked her. Louise gave her a hair brush and hair clips, and from then onwards we started building up the more feminine things she loved. Nicola adored her pink Barbie clothes. Louise would stand her in front of the mirror and encourage her to admire herself. She kept all of her things in a big bag and would go and count every item of clothing to make sure nobody had taken anything away from her.

At first the children seemed a bit overwhelmed by their surroundings, but they liked the fact that there was a working toilet and they could have baths and showers when they wanted them. Baby Kyle loved the bath, he enjoyed it so much that he would scream when you took him out. And the children valued little things like having cereal in the morning. We used the other children in our house to give them a "crash course" in being kids, talking to them about music, football, fashion – all the normal things that children enjoy. We worked on improving their eating habits, using our own children as an example and not making a big deal out of it. We gave the older boys little responsibilities like washing and drying bowls. And we tried to get them into a sense of routines, so they knew that lunch was at 12.30 and dinner was at 6pm.

We were under the impression that the children were only with us for a short time, but the children's case remained with the duty rota officer for the first two or three months so you never dealt with the same social worker. When it became clear that the children were going to be with us for a while, we managed to get Paul and Ewan into school. We found Nicola a place in a private nursery that we paid for ourselves because the local authority wouldn't pay for a nursery placement.

Very quickly all four of them became different children. Within two or three weeks of playing in the garden, their skin colour changed. Nicola's hair, which had been so thin you could see her scalp through it, started to improve. Paul had been so painfully thin when he arrived that he was pear-shaped, like a famine victim, but he started to develop the body of a 12-year-old boy. He soiled for a couple of months after being with us, which professionals felt he'd developed as a means of "comforting" himself. I sat down and chatted with him about this. I approached it by saying that it must be very uncomfortable, and it would be difficult at school, so it was something we needed to work on. Most kids of his age are very aware of their hygiene, so I wanted to build on this. I took him to Boots and we bought products for his hair, shower gel and deodorant just for him, and I made a big thing out of encouraging him to take pride in his appearance. Within a couple of days of having that conversation the problem stopped and never returned.

Paul and Nicola both came with big problems with self-esteem but Ewan didn't seem to have these problems. He was a happy child, just extremely "hyper". He'd be climbing the wall to get outside and when you opened it, he'd be off like a dog. He could run and run in the park. He used to make me laugh because he couldn't run without laughing. He also had the habit of hiding under cars – as a joke – and jumping out at you! He was a lovely, lovely kid.

The baby took a long time to settle into any routine. We put him on the top SMA gold plus* to build him up a bit and then weaned him from semi-skimmed milk onto powdered milk. He was already used to solid food so we kept up with solid baby food. After a couple of weeks he was on an age-appropriate diet which he enjoyed. His weight increase came on considerably. But Kyle had difficulty around sleep times. It was suspected when he came to us that he'd been affected by exposure to drugs and alcohol in the womb, and poor sleep patterns can be a sign of this. You would think a baby would nap two or three times during the day but if you took him up to his cot, he would seriously scream. So we put him on the settee with a couple of cushions and let him sleep like that. As carers you have to be prepared to adapt yourselves and the household to situations. You might try something and it fails, or it has too much impact on other children in the family, so you try different things as well as falling back on what has worked in the past.

Eventually the local authority decided that, because of Ewan's hyperactivity and in order to assist Paul, who needed time to be a

* High-nutrition infant milk product

child, it would be a good idea to have some sort of separation of the children. In the end it was decided that Paul and Nicola would stay with us and the two others would be moved on to another carer. To be honest we'd never felt there were any tensions between the children and we were happy to continue having all of them, but the local authority felt that their needs would be better met by carers giving children more individual time. At times like this you stand there and scratch your head, wondering what you're going to say to the child. It was difficult to explain to these children who had always been together, who had been taken away from one horrific situation and had then started to settle down, why they were being separated. But, as a foster carer, even when you think something is the worst decision for a child, you can't let the child see that. You can't have one set of adults saying this is what we are going to do and another saying we don't think this decision is right. You have to swallow your personal feelings and be seen to be supportive, for the child's sake.

Paul was very concerned about what was happening with his younger brothers. Nicola was obviously worried about the baby but missed Ewan most because Ewan was her playmate and had always made her laugh. Ewan was such an upbeat child, very good for the morale of all four of them. With Paul we could have a slightly more adult conversation and reassure him that he would remain in regular contact with his brothers, and would have the benefit of contact with them throughout his life. We explained that it came back to the situation of adults having to take responsibility, and while, as a child, he may not understand why something was happening, he had to trust adults to do the best for him.

Six months after the children first came to us, a taxi arrived and drove Ewan and Kyle off to their new carer. We'd offered to take the children over ourselves, but we were told that would prove too upsetting. So they left us, being driven away by a police-checked taxi driver – an eight-year-old boy and an 18-month-old baby. All our impulses screamed that it was wrong but we had to go along with it.

So Paul and Nicola remained. Paul was getting on exceptionally
well at school. He was a bright lad and thrived on getting involved
and doing well. Nicola was still at private nursery but preparing to
go into the reception year at primary school; she seemed very settled
at this stage.

When the children first came into care, we'd had lots of calls from
relatives. We had a long conversation with one of the maternal aunts
who put us in the picture about the family dynamics. Apparently the
children's mother was one of five sisters who'd all been sexually
abused by their father. Their mother and one other sister had drug
habits but the rest of the sisters seemed to be getting on with their
lives. The children had regular phone contact with various relatives
and one of the aunts took them to visit their mother in hospital. The
children came back upset, saying that their mother had told them not
to be nice to foster carers and to milk us for anything they could get.
But when their mother left hospital, she disappeared for the next six
months and the children heard nothing from her.

Around this time, Paul's father appeared on the scene. We'd been
aware from early days that Paul had a different father (to that of the
others), who was living in Northumberland. He was living with
somebody else by the time the children's mother was pregnant with
Paul, but never told his partner that he had a child. Paul's father had
been notified of the fact that his son had come into care and decided
to tell his partner – which had caused some strain on their
relationship. Paul had met his dad a few times before and his father
now started to visit on a number of occasions and took Paul and
Nicola out for burgers and bowling. It was encouraging that he was
aware as a parent not to take Paul out without taking Nicola too. On
a couple of occasions he discussed with us the idea of taking Paul to
live with him in Northumberland.

A number of possibilities had been discussed for the children,
including being reunited with their mum, or the possibility of long-
term fostering or adoption. But for Paul, at 12 years old, adoption
wasn't really practical. So social services carried out an assessment

of his birth father, who came through with flying colours, and the decision was made that Paul would go and live with him. We felt this was a good option for Paul and we prepared him for the move with a lot of discussion. Paul's concern was for Nicola and the distance he'd be at from his other brothers. The four children were having monthly contact and weekly telephone contact, and now there was the possibility of Paul moving to Northumberland. Fortunately, Paul's father gave all sorts of undertakings about regular telephone contact and direct contact with the other three.

We made Paul's departure as easy as we could for Nicola. We explained that it was good that Paul could be with his dad, that he'd have somewhere nice to live and be well looked after and she could still talk to him on the telephone. Paul moved to Northumberland, and the day his father was given a full Parental Responsibility Order I took Nicola up to visit them.

I think things could have worked out well for Paul but sadly the children's mother got wind of what was happening and reappeared on the scene. The mother asked for contact with Paul, and Paul's dad said no, as he felt it wouldn't be beneficial. She then started inviting Paul to come to London but not to tell his dad. He'd get to Victoria station and she wouldn't be there to meet him. He'd ring his mother but instead she would ring up social services and tell them that the boy was in London on his own. Social services would then ring his dad, who didn't know what was going on. Sadly, she was a woman who was very good at manipulating situations to her own advantage. We understand that eventually Paul left his father and we believe that he has now returned to live with his mother.

The mother had also asked for regular contact with Nicola. We knew that the mother was supposed to be undergoing a full detox programme and we recognised that it was a difficult period for her. At first it seemed that the mum was happy with us caring for Nicola: she acknowledged that Nicola was doing well in school and seemed pleased with the work we'd done with her. Then the mum got into a relationship at the rehab unit, got involved in a violent incident and was asked to leave.

Whilst the mother was in rehab, one of the aunts from Northern Ireland said she would consider taking Nicola on a Residence Order. The local authority was very keen on this idea. We were concerned at the speed at which the aunt was assessed but we knew Nicola was excited because she knew this aunt well, and had had contact with her on a regular basis. So it was quite an easy process preparing her for the move. However, the placement broke down after two months, apparently because there were problems regarding the aunt's own children who were jealous of the attention shown to Nicola. The London local authority said it was no longer their problem – they were happy for the aunt to turn her over to social services in Northern Ireland. We also knew that the grandfather, who was a Schedule 1 offender*, was offering to have Nicola to live with him. I told the aunt I would go over to Northern Ireland myself and personally take Nicola to social services. But I also involved her guardian, who told the London authority that they would need to arrange for Nicola's care themselves, otherwise he would force them to do so through legal processes.

In the end, the aunt brought Nicola back to London. The local authority said they wouldn't return her to us as they had their own foster carers. We were horrified that they would consider placing her with new foster carers after all she had been through, when we had room and were more than happy to take her back. At that point we let rip and went to senior managers in the local authority. I explained the situation and said I was quite happy to go further up the line and go to court with a solicitor and apply for a Residence Order. The local authority tried to imply that we were maybe getting "a bit too involved" in the case. But that's an old chestnut and we are accustomed to dealing with that. We made it very clear that our

---

* "Schedule 1 offender" is a term used to refer to people who have been convicted of an offence listed in Schedule 1 to the Children and Young Persons Act 1933 – largely offences against children, for example, cruelty or violence.

only concern was the effect this was having on Nicola. The local authority had some very good carers, but what Nicola needed at that point was a bit of stability.

So Nicola came back to us. I had a heck of a job getting her back into the same school, but the headteacher was fantastic. She settled back into life with us for a while. But, as I explained earlier, her mum had been asked to leave her rehab unit, and she seemed to have a personality change once she was back in the community. She started demanding all sorts of things around contact, although she seldom turned up. We knew the mum was living in a bed and breakfast and wanted the local authority to re-house her in a flat, saying she needed this so her children could visit her. Originally we'd been told that consideration would only be given to reunification if the mum completed the whole rehab process fully, which she hadn't. We were also concerned that her new partner was also a drug user. We felt the local authority was very weak-willed and seemed to agree to nearly everything the mother and her solicitor wanted, and the children's needs were way down the line!

We discovered that, when the mum did turn up for contact visits, she always tried to get Nicola alone. She'd then tell Nicola that she shouldn't talk to us, shouldn't tell us anything, that she would soon be back and living with her, so she should talk only to her. We couldn't say anything negative to Nicola about her mum and we couldn't risk having any kind of confrontation with her mum in front of Nicola, but we knew Nicola had lots of worries that she needed to share with us. So we'd say to Nicola, 'Mummy is upset because she can't be with you all the time, and she is saying things that under normal circumstances she wouldn't say. But you have to talk to us about any upsets and anxieties that are worrying you – it wouldn't be fair on you to wait a whole month to tell your mum.' That was the way we got round it and it was quite successful.

Our relationship with Nicola's mum deteriorated because we had to give a report at a meeting about her reliability around contact. We were totally honest and had to say that, from our diary records, she almost never turned up for face-to-face contact, and out of 27 arranged phone contacts she had managed only seven. Then the mum complained that she felt unwelcome in our house, and contact was moved to an external venue.

Eventually a decision was taken that Nicola, Ewan and Kyle were all to be reunited with their mum. The social worker who assessed her was newly qualified and seemed to be utterly intimidated by this woman, who could be quite aggressive. We did make our feelings clear about our worries around the mother's unreliability. We thought that not enough had been done for the mum to prove herself capable of caring for these children. She hadn't completed her detox, she had no money coming in, and nobody seemed to know how she was going to feed the children. We also asked if checks were to be carried out on the mother's new partner who was a known drug user. But we were told that our concerns were irrelevant. There were a lot of things that both we, and the link worker from our agency, felt were badly handled or left unattended.

It raised a real level of anxiety in Nicola when she discovered she was going home. It resurrected for her a lot of feelings that had been dormant since she'd been in care. She began telling us about sleeping on the floor and her mum's men-friends falling on top of her. She started having nightmares. Again, we had to try and appear completely supportive of the decision that had been taken. And it took all the professionalism we had to do so.

Nicola went back to her mother a year ago. We – and Nicola – had been promised contact, but this was denied because we discovered the mother had made 19 complaints about our level of care. Most of these were laughable, but there was one serious complaint that Louise had smacked Nicola. Apparently, when Nicola was questioned about this incident, she changed her story and said Louise had smacked her ten times. When the worker asked why Nicola had originally said it was only once, Nicola replied 'I didn't have my brain switched on'. This was an expression we'd heard

Nicola 's mum use many times, but it's not an expression commonly used by a seven-year-old girl.

The allegations were dropped as no one believed them, but we've never seen Nicola since. We'd been promised a meeting on her birthday but it didn't happen. We've heard that the mother is receiving some help from the family support team, but whenever we've rung up to see how the children are getting on, we get no response.

It was a very sad way for a fostering episode to come to a conclusion. We had to put it behind us and move on as we have other children to look after. But Nicola was with us for nearly three years and we'd built up quite a deep relationship with her. She'd arrived as a half-starved waif with no confidence and become a pretty, happy little girl who enjoyed her school. We hold on to the fact that we know we did a good job with Nicola and her three brothers. We believe we gave them something positive, and helped them through the most difficult time in their lives. It's knowing that you've made some form of difference which keeps you fostering when you've been through an experience like this one.

We're still with our independent fostering provider but we won't take children from that particular local authority again. We're now working with a different local authority where the staff are professionals who look at the wider picture, have an understanding of what these children have been through, and make decisions based on what is best for the child.

Clive and Iain: **Teaching life skills to a homeless teenager**

Providing supported lodgings to a homeless teenager can be quite a challenge, especially if you are unaccustomed to having young people in your home. However, Clive Thompson and Iain Barker have found caring for 19-year-old Ben an enriching experience which they are keen to repeat.

This couple, who are white and live in London, provide supported lodgings through the Albert Kennedy Trust. The Trust is a registered charity which aims to provide accepting, supportive and caring homes for young lesbians and gay men who would otherwise be homeless or living in hostile environments.

Clive and Iain tell their story:

Clive: I saw an advert in the gay papers which asked 'Could you help a homeless teenager?' We are fortunate and have nice lives and helping a young person seemed a good way to give something back. We went along to an open evening hosted by the Albert Kennedy Trust, and discovered that – quite rightly – it was a lengthy process. It took us a year to do the training and they were quite clear that we were free to pull out at any time if it wasn't right for us. The training prepared us for the practical issues of having a young person aged 16 to 21 living in our house, but also explored issues around health and sexuality. For example, you have to think about what is and isn't acceptable in your home with regard to visitors, and what you'd do if you suspected the young person wasn't practising safe sex, or had problems with drink or drugs.

Iain: The organisation has three golden rules – for both the young person's protection but also the carers. No physical punishment, no sexual contact and no secrets. The first two are pretty obvious but the last one takes more explanation. If, for example, a young person visits their family at the weekend then comes back and tells you that a younger sibling is being abused, you can't keep that a secret, however much the young person asks you to. They need to understand that you have a duty to tell your joint case worker.

Clive: After we'd been approved, we waited a while for a young person to be placed with us. The normal process is that you start with introductions, usually in a café with the social worker present so that you and the young person can find out about each other. Then the young person visits your house with the social worker and you maybe go to the cinema or shopping with them. But Ben was 17, looked about 14, had a mild learning disability, and was sleeping on friends' floors or meeting people in clubs and spending the night with them just to have a roof over his head. He was deemed to be at considerable risk and needing an immediate placement. So the process was cut down to just one meeting of an hour. Everyone decided it felt right so it was agreed that the placement should go ahead.

Ben had been in care for part of his life. Apparently he'd been quite a handful to look after, and his mother couldn't manage him. He hadn't seen his father since he was very young and there was a restraining order against his father because of violence. Also, Ben's mother was a devout Christian and apparently found Ben's sexuality hard to cope with. We were told that she had said Ben was putting his brothers and sisters at risk of "infection", which was one of the reasons he felt he couldn't live at home. The young man we met was incredibly shy – not like the Ben we know now, who chats away for hours.

Iain: One of my concerns was that we could be considered a pair of old fuddy-duddies, and how would we relate to a teenager? Clive has nephews and nieces but I haven't had much contact with young people since I was young myself. When Ben came to live with us, I realised that he did all the things I did at his age (and thought my parents wouldn't notice!). We're a non-smoking household – Ben will tell you he hasn't been smoking in our house but he forgets we can smell it. I've realised now how often my own parents must have turned a blind eye when I thought I was cleverly deceiving them. Having Ben with us means that I now know who Bjork is and can recognise some of the contestants on *Pop Idol*. Similarly, Ben can now sit down and watch *Question Time* and take an interest when there's something that affects his life.

Clive: Having another individual in the house for whom you have responsibility is quite a big adjustment. I think we'd had quite hedonistic lives and got used to things like being able to make last minute plans to go away for the weekend. Iain's job requires him to be away some nights and weekends so I have to make sure I am here. Although Ben is now 19, we don't feel it's fair on him to leave him with the responsibility of being in our home alone. Some of his friends are quite strong personalities and it would be all too easy for them to end up back here, resulting in cigarette burns on the carpet and with Ben being left to carry the can for what had happened. So we have to plan our lives carefully, and we are linked with a lesbian couple who provide respite for Ben when we go on holiday.

Also, it's some of the little things you notice most when a young person moves in. Like taking a shower and finding Ben has used the last of the shampoo and never thought to mention it. I've realised that teenagers believe household items replenish themselves by magic.

Iain: Before a young person moves in, your worker visits the house several times to help you identify things that might be a problem. They tell you not to have candles – in case a young person sets fire to the place – and they advise you not to have alcohol around, in case young people help themselves. We banished the candles and put most of our decent wine under lock and key, but we didn't want to live in a prison camp! We always offer Ben a glass of wine if we're having some, or let him have a bottle of wine if he has friends visiting. We want to show him how to treat alcohol responsibly.

Our personal golden rule is no drugs. We have an absolute abhorrence of them. There's a lot of drugs used on the gay scene and it brings people into contact with criminals, and nobody knows what they're being sold. The Trust has firm rules on this and we were clear from the start that we wouldn't tolerate any sort of drug use in the house. However, Ben seems to share our views on this so it's never been an issue.

Clive: We were very naive about the use of the phone. We were advised to put a bar on our phone and have a code that only we could use. However, we told Ben we wouldn't bar the phone but put him on trust. When we received a phone bill for £800 we realised our error. Ben had been phoning friends on mobiles during the day and, with no concept of time, he'd often spent a couple of hours on a call. Ben is still paying us back at £5 a week – which is quite a lot of money for him. It'll never cover the cost of the bill but it's helping him to learn about consequences. We've also learnt from our mistake.

When we have our next placements I think there will be lots of things that we will do differently. We realised that we spoilt Ben quite a lot at the start. We used to take him out to restaurants and we'd lend him money when he was broke. However, we recognised that this wasn't helping him particularly. Now we only take him out on special occasions, like birthdays. He has a weekly food budget and we provide basics, and he buys the rest of his food. To start with we took him to the supermarket and helped him learn about budgeting. Then we left him to do his shopping alone but asked him to show us the receipts so we could see how he was getting on. He seemed to be doing quite well, but then we'd also notice there were some weeks when he'd have nothing in the fridge because he'd spent all his money on clubbing. We still find he's eaten all of a box of chocolates, finished a packet of cup-a-soups or helped himself to some of our wine.

But food is fair game, and we've never had any worries about trusting Ben with money. I can still come home from work and empty my loose change onto the counter or leave my mobile lying around, and know that the next day it will still be just where I left it.

Iain: One of the main concerns about Ben when he came to us was that he'd go home with anyone who offered him a bed. He saw sleeping with people as a practical solution to his problems. He was very vulnerable, but he wasn't a child. Our role was about helping him learn to take better care of himself as a young adult. So the rules had to be adult rules that he could live within.

We were told it was very important to set ground rules and stick with them. One of these rules was that if he didn't come home at night he had to tell us where he was going. Because of his learning disability, Ben doesn't have much sense of time and he would just disappear. In the early days he was often without a mobile and it was difficult to try and keep track of him. Sometimes we wouldn't see him until lunchtime the next day because he'd spent the night out clubbing.

There is an emergency number at the agency if you are worried about a young person. We've learnt to recognise Ben's behaviour patterns and we'd only call the agency if there was something out of character. Fortunately, he doesn't disappear as much now and is better at letting us know where he is going.

Clive: Ben does seem to be quite clued up about safe sex and has attended lots of workshops on the subject. We've heard of carers who've had to manage young people who come on to their friends, flirting outrageously. Fortunately Ben has his own social circle and if we ever bump into him when we are out with our friends, we buy him and his friends a drink, and they soon get bored and drift off.

In the house the rule is that our bedroom and Ben's bedroom are off limits, and we'd never enter his room without asking permission. With physical contact we are very careful – and it's up to him. He sometimes wants to give us a hug or kiss before going out. He's a very affectionate young man and he tells us he loves us and shows us off to his friends as his "foster mummy and daddy"!

Occasionally we've had to step in when we've been out and seen Ben being targeted by older men. But generally teenagers are very shrewd. You notice that they never put their drinks down and they keep a thumb over the bottle. If someone buys them a drink they follow them to the bar to make sure nothing is being slipped into the glass.

Iain: When Ben first moved in, we'd wake up and find all sorts of young people sleeping in our sitting room, but he's learnt to respect our home. He takes real pride in having his own key. We've said to him that if you meet someone special, then it's fine to bring them here whenever you like. But you have to think about who you bring into this house because when you are sharing with other people you need to consider them as well as yourself.

We try not to have too many restrictive rules or fierce recriminations because we think it's important to be open and honest and learn to negotiate and trust people. After all, we are trying to instil in him a sense of how to live. We want to show him a relaxed and trusting atmosphere, and that we have a network of close friends we trust. And that everyone has responsibilities. We get up every day and go to work – even if we've got a hangover or stayed up too late. We hope that if he can take some of these concepts with him when he moves on to live independently, then he'll be able to make sensible choices for himself.

Clive: Ben tends to live in a bit of a fantasy world where he thinks he's going to be "discovered" and become a model or a pop star. It's really good for young people to have dreams but we do worry that he doesn't understand that you have to put in the ground work to achieve your aspirations. We worry sometimes that, seeing our lifestyle, Ben imagines that he's going to be given all this on a plate, and we try and make it very clear to him that we've worked our way up to where we are now.

Finding employment is going to be quite a challenge for Ben, and the Albert Kennedy Trust has arranged for a mentor to help him with his job search. He'd really love a job in a clothes store like FCUK but we've tried to explain that if you want to work in a shop you probably have to start by stacking shelves in a supermarket. We encourage him to be realistic, to try to take advantage of the help and support that's currently on offer. We also try to help him think about how to behave in the workplace. We feel we've helped Ben to calm his behaviour down and to have more understanding of what is appropriate. He used to camp it up and show off in the wrong places, and babble away furiously.

Sometimes people who don't understand the situation say that Ben is just "sponging" off us. As a carer, you have to keep information about the young people confidential, so they don't know the whole picture or understand how difficult it is for someone with Ben's learning disabilities to find a job. However, we do sometimes get a bit frustrated with Ben's attitude ourselves. I think the only time he's thrown tantrums and stormed out is when I've confronted him about his unrealistic attitudes. At one point we made it clear to him that, if he didn't put more effort into looking for work, we would be seeking to terminate the placement. It's difficult for us to impose sanctions – we're not his parents and you can hardly confiscate the stereo of a 19-year-old, so we had to find some way to show him we were serious about wanting him to make better use of the placement.

We also encourage Ben to see his family and to talk to them on the phone. We've had his mother round for a meal and it's good that she's seen where he is living. His mother told us that she's not homophobic and she'd never said any of the things Ben had claimed. We discussed this with our social worker who'd heard a different version. We feel it doesn't really matter why Ben was homeless, or what had caused the stress in the family. What matters now is that Ben has built up a relationship with her again.

Iain: Ben has certainly moved on a lot from the teenager who first came to us. He's been let down a lot in his life and he'd come to expect that people would let him down, but he knows we won't do that. We feel the stability has been very important to him. He'd had some difficult foster placements, with carers who hadn't known what to do with a gregarious, gay young man who dyed his hair pink. With us he can be himself – we're not going to be shocked by what he does. And at the same time we can make it very clear when his behaviour isn't appropriate in a particular situation.

Clive: I think Ben has really blossomed. He's a lovely young man – a really unique little character, who clearly feels secure and more confident. We don't want him to leave us but we understand that our role is to help him move on. We will definitely consider having another young person after this experience.

Abi and Fatmir:
Sharing the experience
of seeking asylum

Life can be very difficult for young people who
find themselves asylum seekers in a country
where they do not speak the language or
understand the way of life. Abi Tesfab uses her
personal experiences as a refugee to empathise
with and care for children from her home country
of Eritrea, and neighbouring Ethiopia. However,
she faced one of her biggest challenges when she
took on Fatmir, a young man from Kosovo who
had never encountered black people before.

Abi Tesfab and her husband Abel came to
England in the 1980s because of war in Eritrea.
Both have considerable professional experience
of working with children and young people. They
currently live in London and foster for a local
authority. They have two birth children.

Abi tells their story:

I was working with some of the London boroughs and coming
across children from Eritrea and Ethiopia who had problems
because nobody spoke their language or understood their
background. Then I met two Ethiopian brothers who were
suffering significantly as a result of this, and that made me decide
I wanted to do something. I said to my husband, if these children
came to us first they wouldn't have this problem. They'd see things
they know, like the coffee being made, and they wouldn't be upset
by people who think that everyone in their country is poor or

starving. So my husband and I applied to be foster carers.

At some stage in our fostering career we said we would take only girls, but then I heard about a 13-year-old Kosovan boy in a children's home. I shuddered inside and thought we must take him. I knew of some children who'd had very bad experiences in children's homes because, however hard staff try, they can't be there all the time for the children, because they work in shifts. I felt a children's home wouldn't be a good place for a child who'd just come from another country.

I telephoned my husband at work and told him about the child and why I thought we should have him. He agreed. But my son said 'Eritrean and Ethiopian children are fine, but why a child from Kosovo?' But my husband and I had worked for a while in Sudan with the Council of Churches and we'd come across people from many other countries. Sudan has so many refugees and the experiences of refugees can be similar. Of course a Kosovan home would have been the best thing, but there was no Kosovan family to take the child and I felt we would be able to help him understand the system and speak the English language.

We didn't know anything about Fatmir's background. He had arrived in the country unaccompanied. When he moved in with us, we had to communicate with him through interpreters because we didn't speak his language. The interpreter came the first day, along with his social worker. This was so Fatmir could ask any questions and so we could tell him basic things about living in our family. The interpreter came several times but we found that when he came Fatmir was always unhappy and confused. Sometimes you realise that an interpreter isn't translating things directly but is trying to put their own interpretation on things, or has their own views about what the child should or shouldn't be saying. When another interpreter came it was much better, and I asked for the same interpreter to come each time. He came twice a week for a couple of months, to help us communicate without too much stress, and to clear up any misunderstandings we'd had since his last visit.

When Fatmir arrived, we were told he had never seen black people before. He had very little with him and I took him out to buy him clothes and pyjamas. In the street he walked far away from me because he didn't want people to see us together. He made it clear he didn't want to be in our house. But I wasn't offended. I said to my children, 'Imagine going to another country and not knowing anything about the language and culture, imagine how he is feeling'.

Fatmir cried so much during the first days. I felt so helpless. I just sat with him and talked to him. I comforted him and explained to him in English all the things that needed to happen and what we would do to help him. I knew he couldn't understand English but he could understand the tone of my voice and body language, that I could feel his sadness. It worked that first time and I did it every time he got upset.

We got Fatmir to start teaching us his language, and we started teaching him English. I told him to watch the younger children's videos, the programmes for under-5s, where you can see the words on the screen. The English alphabet is a Latin alphabet so at least the letters were in his own language.

Children who are far from their own countries and families may have a lot of sadness and confused feelings inside themselves, and you can use different ways to help them express these. Some children can draw well, and when children can't talk about their feelings, they can often express them through pictures. Writing letters and poems is also a good way for children to express their feelings. We encouraged Fatmir to write letters to his family in his own language and that really helped him. We don't push children to tell us about their lives, we are just there to listen if they want to tell us. Some children want to share lots of things with you, some don't. We have sat and cried with children as they have told us terrible, sad stories of how they came here. We never learnt Fatmir's story because he has never chosen to tell us, and we respect that. Some of Fatmir's relatives turned up in this country so he was able to see them, and he probably talked to them about his family. We always say to children: don't bottle up your feelings, tell someone. If you don't want to tell us, then tell someone else you trust.

It's important for a child to connect with their own culture and we took Fatmir to the Albanian Centre, and people there were very supportive towards us. We bought Albanian music and tried to cook Albanian food for him. I asked him through the interpreter about how food was prepared at home and I tried to follow the things he told me. Albanians don't cut their meat and vegetables into small pieces like Eritreans do. So one day we would have food prepared in the Albanian style, and one day in the Eritrean style. When a child comes into your family, you try and adapt your life to make them feel at home, you don't expect them to fit in with everything you do. You have to shift your thinking to accommodate them.

It took time but Fatmir started to settle into our family and he was speaking English well. He still didn't like to be seen with me in the street, and at school parents' evenings he wouldn't be anywhere near me. His behaviour wasn't about hating me. He didn't know me to either love or hate me. He needed time to get to know us and to accept that we were there for him. And he started to blend in with our family. I think it happens because children see you are respecting them and their background. They need to see that you are trying to help them by preparing their favourite food. Also, by making the boundaries clear for them, they feel secure in your family.

There are stereotypes around Kosovan young men being aloof but, like most stereotypes, most of the characteristics aren't true. But Fatmir came from a family where men did very little around the house. I accepted that when he arrived he had more respect for my husband than for me. But by being with us, Fatmir picked up that things are done differently in this society. We have a routine in our family and every Saturday someone does the cleaning. When it was Fatmir's turn, I made sure that he was doing it alongside my son, so he could see the other boy doing it. And he saw that my husband also took his turn.

After four months of living with us, Fatmir asked if I would be offended if he went to another family. He wanted to know if that would hurt us. I said that if it was a Kosovan family that would be a good thing and I would be happy for him, but if it was a white English family then he would find that their culture and language would be just as different as ours. I always tell children that when they are with us I will look after them well, and when they leave us we will continue to think about them but we are not offended if they choose to move. He thought about it and decided to stay with us. I thought it was good that this child was able to consider our feelings and was asking our permission in this way.

Gradually Fatmir became just one of the family, arguing with the other teenagers, but never arguing too much with me. He seemed to have a lot of respect for me. He told his social worker that it was the respect he received from our family for his music, his food and his culture that helped him to settle with us.

Fatmir was never rude at home but sometimes he broke the rules like most young people. But when he was nearly 15, he started truanting from school, displaying aggressive behaviour and getting into fights. It was because of one particular friend who was leading him into trouble. I tried to separate him from this friend because I felt he was a very bad influence on him. This boy was Albanian but he wasn't Fatmir's only Albanian friend. If he had been the only Albanian he knew, there is no way I would have tried to persuade Fatmir to break off the friendship. I know how I felt as an adult when I first came to this country, how badly I needed to speak my language. I needed to sing, or pray or chat in my language so badly I felt I could have died! When I met someone who had Eritrean relatives and went to spend a few days with them, to share the language and eat my own food, it was so wonderful for me.

Many times I sat Fatmir down and talked to him. I found myself telling him all the sorts of advice my own mother gave me, which I'm sure I didn't listen to! I told him that education means a future. I told him that his truanting and misbehaviour wasn't going unnoticed. The police weren't such fools as he thought. As Fatmir's behaviour got worse, we realised that the school was going to exclude him. We decided to withdraw him from school before this happened and find another school for him.

Fatmir's behaviour improved at his new school for a while, but then we were asked to take another Albanian boy. When a new child comes into the family you have to teach them so much. A 15-year-old is as helpless as a five-year-old because he or she knows nothing about the language, the culture, the laws or the education system. You tend to spend a lot of time with them (although I have realised that you have to be careful to give enough time to the other children). Because Fatmir was part of our family we asked him to help by interpreting for us. He became very jealous of the new boy and they had lots of arguments. He'd say that the new boy had it too easy. I tried to explain that it was good to give, and he should try and welcome this boy. Later we found out that the new boy was swearing at Fatmir in his language, so maybe Fatmir had good reason not to like him. With children and young people you should never be too quick to blame one child. You didn't see how much the other child provoked them before they hit them!

Things started to go wrong at school again and we felt that Fatmir needed to understand that he was losing out on opportunities. He was also making it very hard for the other young person to settle. We said to Fatmir that there was no point in him having a foster placement with us if he wasn't going to school. He was reaching 16, and often young people are able to move on at that age. We felt it was best for him to make that move while he still had support from social services. When a young person has got into a pattern of misbehaviour you need to help them break the pattern. It's hard for them to back down in a situation, so a new situation gives them a chance to make a fresh start.

Fatmir was very upset but we said that he would still be considered part of the family, and he could come back and visit us. A child might leave our house but they never leave our family. It was hard for him, but it was the best thing we could have done for him. Fatmir wasn't reaching his potential here but he grasped the new opportunities with both hands. He messed up on some of his chances, but he made good use of his training. He's now doing very well with his own business. He's a brilliant young man.

We had a lot of contact with Fatmir when he first moved on, and he still comes to us whenever he has something to discuss or needs advice or emotional support. Or he just comes to visit, and if he gives us enough notice, we cook his favourite food for him. Young people who leave us know they are always welcome. He knows we are very proud of him and he regards us as his family.

Since Fatmir left us, we've fostered three other Eastern European young people. We learnt about Kosovan culture and we learnt some of the language. Fatmir also taught us something about the country. There is a famous 15th century Albanian hero called Scanderbeg. When children talk about him, we know who he is because we have learnt about him from Fatmir. We hope that when Eastern European children come to us it helps that we have some knowledge of their language, their food and customs, and it doesn't feel quite so strange for them.

Maud, Nathan and Leo:
Dealing with FAS and FAE

The effects of alcohol on a child in the womb can be complex and long-lasting, and often present major challenges for the foster carers who look after children so affected. The effect on children's brain functioning and development, and their impressionability to outside influences, can cause them to behave in ways that those without knowledge of the condition interpret as "strange" or "anti-social". Their carers can be perceived as "bad parents" who are unwilling or unable to control their child's behaviour.

Fostering two boys affected by exposure to alcohol in the womb has made a huge impact on the life of Maud Graham, a single, white carer from London. She has found herself in police stations and the target of neighbour's anger about the children's behaviour. Maud, who has three grown-up children of her own, says that it is very difficult to understand how these children behave until you have experienced living with them!

Note about Foetal Alcohol Syndrome (FAS) and Foetal Alcohol Effects (FAE)

It is commonly accepted that exposure to alcohol in the womb can seriously damage the brain of the unborn child, affecting the child's health and development. Damage is most likely to occur when an excessive amount of alcohol has been drunk. The terms commonly used to describe the effects of alcohol before birth on children are Foetal Alcohol Syndrome (FAS) and Foetal Alcohol Effects (FAE).

Children diagnosed with FAS usually have distinguishing features which include a lack of a filtrum (ridge between nose and mouth), small eye openings, thin lips, and low-set ears. They are often small of stature, fine-boned and can experience medical problems such as heart defects, poor vision, renal failure, etc. However, one of the main impacts on these children seems to be the problems caused to their intellectual functioning. Some of the most common symptoms include:

- *immature and inappropriate behaviour;*
- *impulsiveness;*
- *ADD (Attention Deficit Disorder) and ADHD (Attention Deficit Hyperactive Disorder);*
- *problems with memory and connecting information;*
- *poor judgement of situations and "fearlessness";*
- *limited or no capacity for making "moral judgements".*

It is increasingly accepted that someone with FAS or FAE has very limited control over their behaviour. Many specialist sources of research and information point out that children (and adults) with FAS or FAE find it difficult or impossible to control their behaviour because of their brain dysfunction, especially in stressful situations. It is also accepted that attachment disorders (commonly found in fostered children) combined with FAS or FAE are likely to produce the most difficult types of behaviour.

| **Maud tells their story:**

Nathan came to me in 1987 when he was nine months old. I was told he'd only be with me for two weeks. He was my first placement as a foster carer and was meant to be "straightforward". At the time, there were a lot of pictures on the TV about Romanian babies, and his face was taut like theirs. He only weighed 12 pounds. But nobody had any idea at the time that he'd been affected by alcohol in his mum's womb. They just thought his size and weight were due to his being born prematurely and the results of poor care.

At first, getting Nathan to take solid foods was quite difficult and he sometimes went blue after feeds – that's not so unusual in premature babies. He gained about four pounds in the first month. He started to settle down and really made an attachment to me. If I left the room for a moment he'd cry or try and follow me. His mum was still drinking a lot, so I was told he wouldn't be going home in the near future. But I never realised he was going to be with me for the rest of his childhood!

As he started to grow he was a very bony child, with very knobbly knees and elbows. He was very small in stature. And he had no filtrum, which they say is the classic sign of a child with Foetal Alcohol Syndrome (FAS). I'd take him to a medical appointment and they'd ask, 'How tall was his mum?' They thought he probably had learning difficulties and he also has Reynold's Syndrome which affects the heart and can cause facial abnormalities. And, as he got older, the doctors began to suspect he had ADHD. There were also a lot of pressures on Nathan – his mum had a lot of problems. In the early years she was still drinking and when she came to see Nathan she'd take him to the pub with her, so contact had to be stopped for some time. That upset him a lot. I think Nathan did have all the things they thought he had – like ADHD and learning difficulties – but all these were being compounded by the fact that he'd been affected by alcohol in the womb. But these days, if I saw a child looking and behaving like Nathan, I'd guess straight away that it was FAS.

What I understand by FAS or FAE is that when a woman drinks during pregnancy it can damage the child's brain. These kids don't see the world like other people do. They are unpredictable and impulsive and they can't always help what they do. They can be extremely challenging to care for. You need to make sure you have plenty of help and support, including from a support group if there's one in your area. I had quite a lot of help from family and a few good friends. But you can also lose friends when you care for these children. They don't want you taking a child round to their house who they think is just badly behaved and out of control!

Nathan always banged his head to help him sleep. To this day – and he's now a young adult – he still does it. And he was always "on the go", totally hyperactive. I'd be lucky if I could get him to have any sleep. He had no sense of danger, which I understand is quite common in children affected by FAS or FAE. I had this large wall unit. When Nathan was only two years old, I had left him playing happily on the floor. But when I came back into the room, he had climbed onto a footstool and got himself on top of the unit. When we had meetings with his social worker, if I let go of him for a minute, he'd climb on the back of the sofa and dive-bomb onto my neck. And as he got older he'd climb anything – the bigger the better. He was so agile. You had to be on your guard 24/7. You couldn't leave him for a moment. You had to watch constantly so he didn't hurt himself or other people. We had to keep the windows locked because he'd stand on the windowsill and try and climb out. In his last year at primary school, he went on an adventure holiday which he loved, but one of the neighbours later spotted him about to abseil down our block of flats! I panicked but decided I just had to call him calmly from inside the house. Fortunately he climbed back through the window. You really don't want to live in a fifth floor flat when you have a child like Nathan!

When Nathan started at nursery I had to stay with him. They thought that maybe he had an attachment problem because if I tried to leave him, he'd cry and run out of the room or soil himself. By the time he moved to the reception class at primary school, he seemed a bit better. It always took him longer than other children to adapt to anything new, so we prepared him carefully, and by the time he made the move, he was ready for it. He coped with other

children around him, but only to a certain degree. Children got fed
up with him quickly because the way he played was very immature.
So he'd just move on to the next child. And he was very vulnerable,
very easily led. He was always getting into trouble. He also tended
to be bullied a lot and to become a scapegoat. I used to dread going
to collect him from school because kids would run up to me to tell
me what he'd done wrong that day.

People are so ready to judge you when you have a child like Nathan.
But you have to focus on the child's needs and not worry about what
everyone thinks. I always had someone knocking on my door
complaining that Nathan had done this or that. To other people his
behaviour seemed rude, out of control. Taking him shopping on my
own was a complete no-no because he'd be sliding down the aisles,
knocking people over. On the road, he'd shoot out in front of a lorry
if you didn't keep hold of him all the time. People would make
comments to me that I should keep him under control. Sometimes I
felt like I was failing him because I couldn't manage his behaviour.

There isn't any magic formula when you're caring for a child like
Nathan. You have to try all sorts of approaches, but nothing I tried
worked for very long. I am fairly laid back, and it's important with
these children to focus on the big issues with their behaviour and not
pick on the small things. The only way I coped was because my two
older sons used to come home from work in the evening and take
Nathan off my hands. Nathan has always tended to respond better to
men than women (although he was very attached to me). He saw my
sons as gods! I really don't know how I'd have managed without the
support of my own boys.

The other thing was that Nathan was left-handed and the school
tried to make him right-handed. At home I used to try and follow his
lead, work with whatever was best for him. I looked into things like
getting him left-handed scissors. But the school said it was
important to stick with trying to make him right-handed. For a child
with Nathan's problems, that was a huge hurdle to put in his way.

Nathan never wanted to go to school and many times I had to battle to get him there. I also kept asking for him to be assessed for a statement of special needs. The school put all his difficult behaviour down to naughtiness and the fact that he'd been in care. It wasn't until it started to show in his learning – they saw he wasn't reading and writing properly – that they realised something was wrong. When we eventually went to see a psychiatrist, I ticked all the boxes on the form he gave me. The psychiatrist felt that Nathan definitely had ADHD. He said he'd never seen a child before with such a high score. I broke down in tears, it was such a relief to be able to put a name to his behaviour. Nathan was prescribed Ritalin. I know some people think Ritalin isn't such a good idea for children, but it made a big difference in calming down Nathan's behaviour.

After he was statemented, Nathan was moved to a new primary school for children with special needs. Children like Nathan normally hate change, but he loved the new school. The staff were wonderful. But everyone still thought that he had the potential to grow out of his ADHD and start to blossom. What they didn't realise is that children with FAS tend to hit a stage where their learning "sticks", after which they don't seem to be able to progress. They're always behind other children. At five Nathan was at the level of a three-year-old; at nine he was functioning like a six-year-old.

When Nathan was about eight I adopted him. I'd started off as a short-term carer but he hadn't been able to go back home, and when they looked for an adopter they couldn't find anyone to come forward for him. It was also decided that, with his problems, it would be damaging to move him after he'd been with me for so long. When it was agreed that he would be staying with me, I was moved from a fifth floor flat to a ground floor flat, for Nathan's safety.

When he was about 11 years old, Nathan was finally diagnosed with FAS. He hadn't coped well with the move to secondary school and the psychiatrist he'd been seeing regularly had died. I felt we weren't getting enough support to help him. I was looking up everything I could find about ADHD and trying to find support groups in the area. The school suggested another doctor who they felt had a lot to offer kids with ADHD. But when we saw the doctor, he said that Nathan had FAS as well as ADHD. I asked 'What does this mean?' But I was just told to go on giving him the Ritalin.

I looked up everything I could find about FAS. They know a lot about it in the United States, but over here there was little knowledge and even less support. You don't want to put labels on children, but at the same time knowing what is wrong helps. If you have information about FAS, then you can be armed properly to deal with it. For example, you realise that confronting a child with FAS doesn't help, because they do things without any thought. Nathan once picked up a hammer because a boy did something to upset him. Leo, the child I'm fostering now, also has FAS and he says it's like someone else takes you over.

They say about FAS that the kids have it, but the whole family lives it! And as Nathan grew up, we started to really feel the effects on the whole family. To other children Nathan was always different, so he was someone they could target. And what Nathan wanted more than anything was to belong. In order to be part of the group, Nathan would do anything other kids wanted him to do. So he'd be the one that got into trouble for putting a brick through a window. If he had money on him, kids would turn him upside down. I even took one boy to court because he was stealing Nathan's money, punching him and setting fire to him. One time Nathan was kicked round a field full of dog muck. But whatever they did to him, Nathan wanted to be part of the gang. I know most of these other kids had their own problems – and many of them have ended up in prison since then – but Nathan was always the one who got into trouble because he stood out, because he looked different.

You can't keep a growing lad cooped up all the time, you have to let them go out and mix with other children. So I used to stand outside the flat, keeping an eye on him. I even learnt to drive so I could go out and look for him. I tried hard to get him into clubs and places where he could meet new friends, but it never worked. He just wanted to be part of what was happening in our neighbourhood. Children and young people like Nathan don't think about the consequences of their actions. They can't make those sorts of connections. They also take on the personalities of the people around them. So, if they're with loud, reckless people, they behave in the same way. I've been to the police station with Nathan about three times. I've had to tell the police what is wrong with Nathan and I even got the doctor to write a letter to explain his condition. He was once cautioned for breaking three milk bottles. He had no idea why he'd done it, he had just acted on impulse. One woman pushed Nathan down the stairs because he'd annoyed her. One of our neighbours told me she'd almost hit Nathan with a dog lead because of something he'd done. I said, 'It's a pity you didn't, because then I would have taken you to court!' People need to realise you can't treat a young person in that way.

If you give Nathan love, he gives you love back. But if you give him ignorance, he gives you twice as much ignorance back. He cares about people who respect him, but people think it's OK to swear at him and treat him like dirt. With Nathan, it takes a long time to get new ideas into his head. He needs things to be in order, so he can understand them. I tried to teach him ways to stop him losing things, to get things ready on time for school, and how to manage his temper. Of course, he winds me up sometimes but he says, 'Don't put me down like everyone else, you are the only one I can rely on!'

He can be a very sensitive boy. There's such a lovely side to him. I remember once I was having problems with my youngest son. I was talking to him on the phone and I was crying. Nathan got a chair and sat down beside me and held my hand. After I put down the phone, he gave me a hug. And I remember Nathan – the boy who everyone thinks is so awful – was so gentle with a baby we had fostered. The baby was teething and Nathan, who is such a night creature, heard him crying and went in, changed and fed him. He then came and told me what he'd done. When I checked the baby, I found that Nathan had done everything right. Even now, when that baby – who is now a little boy – comes back to visit us, Nathan takes him to play on the swings and is so gentle with him. I love Nathan to death. If I didn't, I don't know why I'd put up with his behaviour. And besides, if I turned my back on him, who'd have had him?

At his specialist secondary school they wanted to move Nathan to the EBD* unit but it's all lock-and-key stuff and I felt that wasn't going to help him. I really felt they weren't looking at his needs properly. They said that it was up to Nathan to ask for his Ritalin tablets, not their responsibility to give them to him. But what child goes and asks for tablets! If he had a tantrum, they'd phone me to collect him. There was never two days when they didn't ring me to take him home. So he started being excluded for long periods. But if a young person gets the message that, by behaving in a certain way, they'll get sent home from school, they soon learn that it pays to put that behaviour on. Fortunately, I had a really good relationship with the education welfare person, who understood the problems I was dealing with.

I wanted Nathan to move schools before he was permanently excluded. But the Education Department was so slow. I contacted the Citizen's Advice Bureau and was told by their solicitors that Nathan had been badly let down. I got to the stage where I was getting so low myself that I felt I couldn't get much lower. But I realised I had to shake myself up because it wasn't helping anyone. I had to go on the rampage for Nathan's sake. I had to go on fighting the battles for Nathan's sake: battles with the young person and battles with school and authority. I'm currently thinking about starting a support group for other carers and parents of children with FAS.

Nathan tried to return to school at one stage, but he'd had a spurt of growing while he was away so wasn't wearing the school jumper.

* Emotional and Behavioural Difficulties.

They said that because he wasn't in full uniform he couldn't stay in school, and sent him home. I went ballistic! I became a school governor to speak out for children like Nathan. Schools are too ready to exclude children without looking at the child's needs and understanding their problems.

With children like Nathan you have to be imaginative and keep looking for new ideas to manage their behaviour. Sometimes taking away things like possessions or privileges works, but at other times Nathan just doesn't care about these. I've taught him different ways to try and control his temper. And I've had to adapt as he's got older. When he was younger, I could remove him into another room to cool off, but I can't do that now. So instead, when he starts pacing and punching the wall, I take the younger child I'm fostering and we go off to the shops. Usually by the time I get back, Nathan has calmed down and he tells me he's sorry. I don't think he'd ever hit me but he's strong and impulsive and if you go head-to-head in an argument with him you can't guarantee what he might do.

Nathan really struggled through secondary school. Fortunately, at the moment, he has some older friends who are very sensible, and who've known him for a long time. One of them has taught Nathan about care mechanics and is taking him into work with him, when he can. Nathan's now 17 and he's still very vulnerable. He's been smoking and drinking a lot and he gets very depressed. He won't see his psychiatrist and so I went to see him myself. The psychiatrist felt we should be looking at independent living for Nathan. But nobody seems to know where I'd find an appropriate scheme. But whatever I do find for him, Nathan has to believe that it's his idea, that it's something he is doing of his own accord. So far he has stayed out of serious trouble, but I do worry about the future. At the moment, if he's arrested the police have to tell me. But when he's an adult and if I'm not there, will he be able to tell people that he has damage to his brain which affects his behaviour?

A couple of years ago I was asked to foster Leo, who was also eventually diagnosed as having FAE. It's not the full syndrome but

FAE has many of the same effects (as FAS) on the brain's functioning. Leo had been in care since he was 18 months old. His mother had gone on an alcohol binge but was in total denial that she had a problem. He was so depressed at being taken away from her. He'd seen a lot of violence in his family and experienced neglect. It took him a while to settle down with us.

He had the classic appearance – small of stature and bony with big kneecaps. His filtrum wasn't well developed. And Leo banged his head like Nathan did. It didn't matter what the surface was – soft furnishing, wood or concrete – he'd bang his head viciously against it. He actually knocked some of my teeth out when he head-butted me when he was about 19 months old. The child psychiatrist we had access to through CAMHS* felt that Leo was communicating his frustration in this way because he couldn't talk, especially when he'd seen his mother. He was so upset that he couldn't go back to her.

We got him into a group at a family centre so he could start to socialise with other children. He wasn't bothered by me leaving him – as long as he knew I was coming back, he was fine. I made sure I always dropped him off on time and collected him on time. If by any chance I couldn't be there or was going to be late, I'd prepare him for it beforehand, or I'd make sure that I'd contacted his key worker so she could explain to him why I'd been held up.

Leo was quite an aggressive child. I think he was acting out some of the violence he'd seen at home. He was quite aggressive towards other kids, and I've been kicked, bitten, punched and head-butted by him. By the time he returned to his mum, when he was three years old, his behaviour had changed so much. He was becoming a lot calmer and reaching his milestones. His aggression had lessened. He still had temper tantrums but I'd learnt how to stop him going full pelt by distracting him – although sometimes you couldn't divert him and he needed to go through the full temper tantrum. I found that things that worked for Nathan often also worked with Leo, but

* the Child and Adolescent Mental Health Service.

not every time. It was always a learning process. Each child is different and Leo isn't Nathan.

Sadly, going home to his mother that first time didn't work out. One day I got a phone call saying his mum had gone on another drinking binge and could I come and pick him up from nursery. After that, he didn't see her again for about three years, which really upset him. When Leo came back to me, his behaviour was all over the place. After all those experiences he was back to square one. And in the meantime, we were fostering a baby and my granddaughter was with us quite a lot. He was so very jealous of anyone who had anything to do with me. He was very angry and he was throwing things about. Just like Nathan, he had no sense of danger and was always on the go, and when you told him "no" he would just lose it.

We had a big pine coffee table and one day, Leo climbed onto it and jumped on it until it smashed. When he gets into a "paddy" he just lashes out. One time I tried to take him out and he refused to put on his shoes. He told me he was going to scream – which he often does. He kept the screaming up for about 20 minutes. So we decided it would be best to take him in the car. He was pinching me and refusing to put his seatbelt on. Then he picked up something and hit me with it, and started kicking me. So I took him out of the car and sat him on the wall and told him that he wasn't going anywhere until he calmed down, which he eventually did. On another occasion, he threw a brick at my brand new car and broke both my wing mirrors.

It got to a stage with driving where I felt so unsafe that I thought I might injure or kill us or someone else. Leo would be doing handstands, jumping backwards and forwards on the back seat, trying to put his hands over my eyes or trying to pull on the handbrake while I was driving. So I eventually insisted on the local authority providing a cab to take him to school.

Another time he started throwing Christmas decorations at me because I said I was going to take down the decorations. And he screamed like I was killing him. He turned the Christmas tree over and threw everything around. A woman from the next block of flats came knocking on the door, saying she was going to call social services because I was clearly abusing the child. I said, please come in and talk to this child. Ask him why he is screaming and whether I have hurt him. He quite calmly explained that he was screaming because I'd taken the decorations down when he wanted them up.

Things were very difficult for Leo. He missed his mum badly and at one point his agency thought they'd found him a new family. So I started preparing him for this, which I've done with other kids. He took it very badly and smashed up his bedroom. He said he didn't need a new family because he had us. Then I found out that the couple who were going to take him had pulled out several months before and no one had told him. That's so unfair when you're looking after a child with Leo's behaviour problems.

There was also the time he put his foot through the bedroom window in a rage. And he also told his teacher he wasn't coming home to me because I'd strangled him. I asked him to show her what I'd done to him. He grabbed the teacher's wrist! Earlier that day I'd had to take hold of his wrist firmly. But he can so easily exaggerate things. You could find yourself being accused of all sorts! If you touch his face he might say you'd "cut" his face, or if you touch his arm you've "injured" him.

I can tell now when Leo is "winding up". He will come up to me and look at me with a certain expression on his face and say something like "you fat chicken". Or I'll go into his bedroom in the morning and his eyes will snap open and he'll say, 'Get my breakfast'. I just play it down, say something like 'Good morning, Leo', and try to get his medication into him before he erupts.

Leo was diagnosed with FAE about three years ago. In the United States, there's quite a range of drugs used to help these children. But here, there's no medication that a child can take at an early age. Leo has now been on slow-release Ritalin for a year. That's to treat the ADHD aspect of the FAE. What a difference it makes! I've devised a system where I wake him up at seven in the morning and give him his tablet and then he goes back to sleep for a while. By the time he gets up, his behaviour is manageable. It means we don't have problems like the cab driver refusing to drive him to school because he's having a paddy. He's kicked the driver in the past and understandably they're not too keen to take him when he behaves like that.

Recently he changed schools and staff at the current school say he has settled in well. Getting him to do his homework is a nightmare but he's bright as a button. I do worry though that he may just hit a brick wall and his development will "stop", which sadly is quite common for children with FAE.

At the moment, the plan is for Leo to return home to his mother. We are taking things very slowly, doing shared care with him, and Leo goes to stay with his mother for short periods. Leo is very wary. He knows that his mum may not be able to help returning to her drinking. I know his mum really wants to do the best for him, but I am worried that she hasn't been given a ground floor flat. Children like Leo aren't safe in anything above ground level. He's jumped out of my windows – even opening the safety locks – and he's likely to do that at any height.

I really don't know if things will work out for Leo and his mum. He has said to me that he doesn't want to live with her, he just wants to visit her. He has asked me if he will still be part of my family, and of course I can't say no! He knows he'll still be able to phone me and see me. I do believe his mum will give it her very best shot to make it work for him, but I don't know if that will be good enough because there are so many hurdles in her way, and he's not an easy child to care for. I know she feels a huge amount of guilt about the way her drinking has affected him and she tends to spoil him, though he's a child who needs very clear boundaries and systems. I hope I'm wrong, and it can work out. I will offer them all the support I can. She is reading everything I give her about FAE, and I know she has his best interests at heart and loves him to pieces.

11

Vaughan and Sian:
Helping a 'lovely lad' with a darker side

A genuine liking for a child, teamwork and a sense of humour can be the saving factors for a very difficult foster placement. Without these, husband and wife Vaughan and Sian Jenkins believe they would never have been able to care for Declan, an accident-prone young man with learning difficulties, no sense of danger, and inappropriate sexual behaviour.

Vaughan and Sian Jenkins from west Wales have been fostering for eight years, and are both full-time carers. They work for a local authority scheme doing task-focused work with children with challenging behaviour, who are often at risk of going into custody or secure units.

| **Vaughan tells their story:**

Declan was a lovely lad. He had a lot of problems – and still has – but there was something about him that you took to . . . The thing about fostering is you don't know what is round the corner, what problems children are going to bring to you, so if you can latch onto something likeable in the child's personality, it makes it easier to care for them. With Declan, you went not just that extra mile for him but 50 times round the block! He had endearing characteristics and infuriating habits. I drove him for a contact visit once and he sang 'Roses are red, violets are blue' non-stop for 120 miles. By the time I got there I was starting to foam at the mouth a little!

Declan was 12 when he was sent to us because of behavioural problems. He was the product of one of the most neglectful families I've ever come across. Most of the family members had learning difficulties. They used the bathroom for storing dirty clothes and used a commode in the sitting room. Not surprisingly, he had poor personal hygiene. When Declan was six years old, he and his brother were recovered by the police at 2am playing on the road, wearing T-shirts in the middle of November. But the boys didn't come into care for a few more years. By the time he came to us, he'd been in care for about a year. He'd had to be moved because he'd been found masturbating over his brother.

We'd heard that, if the previous foster carers censored Declan in any way, he'd hang out of the bedroom window, shouting 'Help! Help! Call the police, they're killing me'. One of the neighbours had obliged. But when you are living in a farmhouse like ours, you can shout all you like and no one's going to hear you. The first time he hung out of the window shouting, it lasted maybe four hours, the next time three hours. When he realised it wasn't going to get him anywhere, it burnt itself out as a behaviour.

If you left Declan next to the fridge he would keep raiding it till it was empty. He had no "off" button as far as eating was concerned. He also used to soil himself incredibly. It would have been nice if someone had told us that before he moved in! Finding a heap of dirty underwear stashed at the bottom of his wardrobe wasn't really the surprise I wanted on Boxing Day afternoon. He'd wipe his bottom with his underpants and flush them down the loo – we have a septic tank so you can imagine the fun that caused! But we managed to sort the soiling problem out over a year. However, he went on wetting the bed throughout his stay with us.

Declan was also incredibly destructive. You'd buy him loads of Christmas presents and they'd all be broken by Boxing Day. You'd buy him a Walkman and a day later it would be trashed. That boy could break an anvil. You'd hear a whoosh of water and know he'd flooded the bathroom again. He could destroy a computer in minutes. We were in a nature reserve – which I hesitate to say too much about in case they sue me – and he went up to a computer and started clicking on all the boxes. When we left, there was a guy rebooting the whole thing because Declan had wiped Windows off the system.

We kept pigs at that time. Declan turned a hosepipe on the piglets . . . they could have died of hypothermia. We gave him a hard time for doing this, explaining how bad it was for the pigs to get cold and wet. Not long afterwards some of the pigs got out of their field and Declan found them in the rain, and decided to invite them into the house. You cannot believe the amount of damage two 300-pound adult pigs can do in the living room! But how could you give the boy a row when his answer to why he'd done it was 'But it's wet outside!' We had a term for situations like that. We used to say 'It's been Declan'd'.

Not long after he came to us, Declan went to a neurologist as he had a tremor and problems with motor skills. The neurologist was very dismissive, saying Declan would never be able to do anything. But we bought Declan a bike and stabilisers. As I went outside to fit the stabilisers, Declan came past riding the bike! He'd learnt to ride in 20 minutes. I wanted to video it and shove it up the neurologist's backside. How can people be so negative about children?

Before we started fostering, Sian and I had run homes in the community for adults with learning disabilities. So we don't believe in limits, we push children that little bit harder to see what they can do. We showed Declan that there are no boundaries. We had higher expectations than other people and he met them. If you plant the idea then a child turns it over in their head and begins to think of themselves as someone who can achieve.

Declan achieved all sorts of things while he was with us. He got a Royal Yachting Association Qualification and was competent to take a small dinghy out on his own. We'd introduced him to the Sea Cadets but his sense of danger was so lacking that they said they

couldn't have him because he'd been about to walk off the harbour
wall and fall 20 foot into the sea. But we're very fortunate as there's
a set of schemes for local young people and Declan went on a taster
day. The sailing came out of this. The scheme immediately put in
one-to-one support for him, and as he learnt to do more and more
things for himself, the one-to-one support was withdrawn. Declan
was doing very well in education and the school put a lot of effort
into helping him. Despite his moderate learning disabilities, he
studied for four GCSEs, which he'd probably have passed. When he
came to us he could not write his name; 12 months later he was
reading the Goosebumps book series. We have an expectation that
all our children will attend school and do their best, and with Declan
that paid off. And people like the receptionist in social services
would comment on how much Declan's behaviour had improved,
she'd say he'd become much politer. Other people commented on
the way his concentration had improved.

There was also a very dark area in Declan's behaviour which was
harder to deal with. He would target young children for sexual
activities. Our children were perfectly safe with him, but every so
often he'd see a child and a light would go on in the back of his
head and he'd be gone. We were on a beach at a fireworks display
and he spotted a particular child. You could just tell what was on his
mind. There were four foster carers on the beach that day and we all
arrived at the same moment because we felt there was something
about the way he was behaving which made us all feel
uncomfortable. When Declan told us that he and this child were just
going to the toilets, our immediate reaction was 'No!'

We went camping in north Wales and Declan was playing with a
group of kids and everything was fine, and then this small boy
turned up. The next thing we know this small child is saying, 'I'm
going to Declan's tent and we're having a special party with disco
lights'. I took Declan to one side and said to him, 'Whatever you are
planning, just think about it – would this child's father be giving you
sweets for doing this, or chasing you with a baseball bat?' Declan

was quite reflective and then said it would be the baseball bat. So I said to him, 'What are you going to do? Do you still think it's a good idea to take this child to the tent?' And Declan said 'No'. But then 30 seconds later I heard him saying to the child, 'When we have the special disco party . . .' So at that point we had to step in. It was as though Declan just couldn't help himself – the behaviour seemed to be ingrained.

It took us a while to work out why only some children triggered this behaviour in Declan. With the help of our link worker it clicked. They were all like his younger brother. He'd clearly been involved in some very inappropriate sexual behaviour and had a very mixed-up approach to sex. If we brought home a clothes catalogue, all the ladies' lingerie pages would disappear, and reappear all over Declan's bedroom. He was looking at a picture of a scantily dressed woman one day and he said to me, 'She wants it'. So I said, 'What does she want, Declan?' and he explained quite graphically what he had in mind. So I asked why he thought that. He said, 'I've seen women look like that . . .' 'Who?' I asked. 'My mum', he said. I remember thinking, OK, better take this one carefully. So I said, 'Where did you see your mum looking like this?' thinking maybe he'd spied on her in her bedroom. And Declan replied, 'In the living room. She was just going to do it with her boyfriend.' So I asked what he was doing at the time, and he replied, 'I was on the sofa watching *Neighbours* with Gran.' You just had this awful image of people shifting around to try and see the television while this couple went at it hammer and tongs in front of them . . . We already knew his mum was quite unable to cope. I'll never understand why social services hadn't intervened earlier. This woman had already done time for sexual abuse and neglect.

We have a number of support staff who work with us. One day, one of these women was driving and her dog was in the back of the car making strange noises. She adjusted the mirror and saw what Declan was doing to the dog! Declan's family had a dog and he tended to repeat things he'd seen before. We wondered if we needed to call a dog protection conference! Sometimes the only way is to use humour to turn a situation around, otherwise you'd never be able to cope with the things you have to deal with or listen to.

Incest had been a way of life in Declan's family, going back generations. Declan was close to his gran but she let things be done to her children and grandchildren because that was what was done to her. She thought it was normal. We speculated that Declan's "uncle" was his father *and* his grandfather. Hopefully, having got Declan out of this cycle of abuse, we've gone some way to helping him break this behaviour pattern.

With a child like Declan you have a list of the things you have to change – the "As" are the urgent things, the "Bs" are the things you'd like to change, and the "Cs" are the things you'd change in an ideal world. You start by working on something very small and move towards bigger things. Declan really wanted to please, and if a child wants to be well regarded, you are on to a winner! What you try to do is establish the behaviour you want and cut across negative behaviour. You then reward children for the positive behaviour. So you say, 'If you do this, then you can have your stereo on tonight,' rather than 'If you do that, then I'll take your stereo away.' These are children who have never succeeded, never been praised. All of a sudden they are making discoveries about themselves, finding out what they can do. Declan could see himself as someone who could steer a dinghy and ride a bike. He was not just someone with a learning disability but someone who could do things. It gives the child a sense of self-worth. I spoke to Declan recently and he'd got a job in a shop. But he'd walked out because he wasn't being paid properly, they'd made assumptions that he was too stupid to realise they were using him. Some people might think that's a bad thing but I see that as a good thing. He had enough sense of his own value to realise that people were trying to take advantage of him. When you have no sense of self-worth, other people can do things to you.

In all our work, Sian and I foster as a team. We have daily planning meetings because you need to use consistent approaches. All

children will try to divide and conquer when they're trying to get
their own way and you can't allow wedges to be driven between the
two of you. You need to be singing from the same hymn sheet when
it comes to working with these children. Whatever one of us is
doing, the other does the same, although sometimes with certain
provisos and modifications around things like safe care. And we
sometimes come across children in whose families women are the
downtrodden members, and the males are very dominating. So we
try to compensate for that by showing them something different.
When the child comes to me to ask something, I'll say 'Go and ask
Sian'. So the child sees that the power balance is equal. Despite
having some problems around women, Declan had real respect for
Sian. At one stage, we had a very institutionalised, tough lad staying
with us. 'If Sian tells me to do something I'll just tell her to f***
off', this lad announced. Declan looked at him, incredulous: 'Are
you mad?' he said.

You could see Declan was learning to be more aware of himself and
of dangerous situations, and the need to self-regulate. With Declan
there was always a bit of him that was like a very young child – a
moment of impulse and he was gone. So you had to say 'Stop' and
mean it. It's very simple stuff, but it delivered for him. You had to
put in very firm boundaries. For Declan this was razor wire with
towers and guards at every checkpoint! But this helped him to
manage many aspects of his behaviour. You could see the results.

Declan's sexual problems were the most difficult aspect to work
with. You could talk Declan out of doing many things but with the
sexual impulses he just didn't seem to be able to control himself.
He'd had a fantastic social worker who knew all about his history
and his family, but after she left, Declan's case was unallocated. We
felt that Declan needed specialist help but there was no one to turn
to and nothing available. Eventually, Declan was given a new social
worker, but she didn't seem to have a clue how to work with a child
with his problems. She seemed frightened of him. Eventually, I
phoned Ray Wyre myself – he's an expert on working with abusers.

He spent an hour talking to me on the phone and he really understood what we were worried about. He said, that is always how abusive situations happen, you get a feeling that something is wrong from the way a person is behaving but you don't know exactly what, so you have to go with your gut instincts.

But the day I spoke to Ray Wyre was the day everything came to a head. Declan had told his new social worker that Sian had hit him when he was in the car. One of our other young people who'd been in the car at the time told the worker that was a load of rubbish. Good practice suggests that the social worker should have written the allegation down, together with the words of the other young person, and discussed this with her line manager. But she didn't. So when – at a statutory review – Declan blurted out to the Chair of the review that Sian had hit him in the car, everything went into circus mode. The conference was abandoned and child protection procedures were put into place. Declan's social worker was like a rabbit caught in the headlights. She never mentioned that she'd already been made aware of this allegation.

Nobody thought about why Declan was making these allegations. We'd had a young woman placed with us for a while and Sian became aware that Declan was stealing some of her soiled underclothes for fetishistic behaviour. I'd said to him, 'If this girl finds out you are doing this, she is going to rip your head off, boy!' She did find out – and it was quite spectacular! She made a formal complaint to her social worker who took it very seriously. Declan was required to attend a meeting and write a letter of apology. At the same time, another young woman in the area got her own flat after she'd made allegations against her carers. I think Declan put these things together and thought that if you made allegations people took you seriously and you got your own flat.

But they had nowhere to put Declan and they sent him to his uncle's – the one we always suspected was also his father and grandfather. Under the uncle's influence, Declan went into overdrive. He claimed that we'd systematically tortured him and that I'd chased him round the house with an axe. I remember my link worker sitting there with her head in her hands as her manager confronted me with these stories. She couldn't believe this woman wasn't challenging Declan about these allegations. Eventually, Declan's social work department moved him to a residential unit in the Midlands. It was very sad because it was Declan who lost out, and he didn't get a chance to do the GCSEs he'd been studying for.

We felt very demoralised at the time. Declan's first social worker had worked alongside us every step of the way and she'd been replaced with a worker who seemed helpless about what to do. If a child makes allegations, it needs to be handled properly and seen through to some kind of outcome. If wild allegations aren't challenged, there's a strong risk factor for anyone who comes into contact with the young person in the future, because it gives the message that you can say anything you like and there won't be any reprisals.

I really miss having Declan in our family. But he was in touch as soon as his social work department let him phone us. For us it's very important to stay in touch with young people who have lived with us – it's part of the fostering role you are not paid for. Declan didn't realise what making those allegations had put us through. He just rang up and it was 'Hi, how are you?' As far as he was concerned, everything was OK.

Declan still calls us whenever there's anything major happening in his life. When he was seriously assaulted, it was us he rang at 11.30 at night. Another time we got a call and it was Declan saying 'I've run away. I nicked some money and they're going to do me for it.' So Sian said to him, 'Do you think running away is a good idea? Wouldn't it be better to go back and face things?' And he agreed it would be better than sleeping in the bus shelter. We rang his residential unit and asked 'Have you lost someone? We think you'll find you have a little knock on the door in a while . . .'

You may feel sad about the way a placement ends, but with

fostering you need to look at things in the long term. It's about the way you feel when the phone goes at midnight on the new millennium and it's a young woman, who'd been a very difficult placement at the time, ringing to wish you a happy new year. You can't put a price on that!

It was incredibly hard work, caring for Declan. It was probably one of the most difficult pieces of work we've ever done, but also one of the best. There were negatives, but there were more positives. Declan made a lot of progress while he was with us. The rewards of fostering aren't what you achieve but what the young people achieve for themselves, and knowing you've been part of that. Declan is not in prison and he has got himself a bit of a life. He's never going to be mainstream, but if we did enough to contribute to him being able to get a job and hold things together in the community, then we've done alright. You can't help but worry that the darker impulsive side of him will come to the surface, but apart from that, I think he will be alright. He's an endearing character and fondly remembered by everyone here.

12

Therese and Joanne: Bringing life back under control

Helping an "out of control" teenager from a secure unit re-establish themselves in society is a daunting task. Although the experience has been challenging – and at times heartbreaking – Therese Cannon feels that enabling Joanne to come to terms with her past has helped this very volatile young woman make positive steps towards independent living.

Therese and Jim Cannon from Glasgow have two children of their own. Therese worked in a residential school for teenagers before hearing about the NCH Foster Care Community Alternative Placement Scheme (CAPS). They applied to foster for this specialist project which aims to keep "high tariff" young people out of secure accommodation and residential schools. They have had two long-term placements and many short-term placements of young people through CAPS.

Therese tells their story:

We met Joanne when she was 11 years old and living in a secure unit. She was there because she was placing herself at risk – she'd picked up on her parents' drug misuse and was going to houses where there was heroin abuse. She'd been in care from an early age and had been in lots of foster placements and residential homes. She kept running away and was considered to be "out of control". Her social worker explained to us that finding her foster carers through the CAPS project was a "last-ditch attempt" to try and keep her out of the penal system.

When we met Joanne her first words were to us were, 'I've been waiting for a family for eight years. Will you be my mum and dad?' I explained that she already had a mum and dad, and said, 'We'll be Therese and Jim. That's what everyone calls us.' Joanne was on a secure order, so she was with her worker when we first met her. But this order was then removed. She came for some overnight stays and then a weekend and we had a chance to say "yay" or "nay" to the placement, as did she. We decided to go ahead and she moved in.

At first Joanne was very eager to please and the front she put up was very false. Her moods soon started to show through. Inside she was a very angry girl, very volatile. Her mum had died because of drugs and there were questions about her dad being involved in her death. Joanne would say, 'If it wasn't for my dad, I wouldn't be in care'. Her mum had also had a lot of influence on her. She'd say to me, 'My mum told me to spit on foster carers and bite and hit'. If she was caught doing something wrong, then she'd say that was the result of her doing what her mum had told her to do. This continued for a year and a half, when Joanne put all responsibility for her actions on what her parents had said and, according to her, her mum and dad were never wrong!

It was important to talk through with Joanne the consequences of her actions, as well as being very firm about where the boundaries lay. When she arrived, she'd say to me, 'I stay out until 11pm 'cos that's what I'm used to.' I'd say, 'No, you'll be home by 9pm. If you return at 9pm, then we will discuss whether you can sometimes stay out a bit later.' If she did stay out late, often for a few days in a row, I would tell her she was grounded. She'd say to me, 'When did you make up that rule?' But I'd explained that to her from the start. You had to be very clear with her about what would happen if she broke the rules.

I found that grounding her was the best sanction because she loved doing activities. We introduced her to lots of different clubs – skating, youth club, dancing, guides, line dancing, swimming – she tried them all. She'd say, 'Take away my pocket money but don't ground me'. She would get very angry and shout and swear. You just had to stay very calm. I don't think she was used to people staying calm with her.

I remember that one day I grounded her because she'd stolen cigarettes from my sister-in-law's house. We're a big family and one of my sisters acted as her respite carer, and she often visited other members of my family. She swore it wasn't her who had taken the cigarettes, and she was very convincing. Whenever you confronted her with anything she always denied responsibility. I spent an hour talking to her about the incident, trying to relate it to things she would understand. I asked her how she'd feel if I went to her nana's house and stole from there. I explained that we wanted her to be with us but we didn't want to have to follow her around and that my sister-in-law wouldn't want her to visit if she continued to steal.

Sometimes when she was flying into a rage she'd inform me that she'd had enough and was moving out. I would let her get on and pack her bags. She'd be waiting for me to crack and yell at her that she couldn't leave but I'd just say 'On you go...' I'd then inform her worker that she had packed her bags. I remember after one night when she'd run away from the house I explained that she needed to understand how her actions made her lose out on things. I told her that, as a result of her actions, she must spend the evening in and iron her clothes. Some friends came round and I discovered she was talking to them out of the window. I said OK, just talk to them for five minutes. But she ran out of the house again. Jim had to go out and look for her. She came back bawling and screaming abuse at him. Eventually she said she was sorry but later in the evening she was trying to get out again. You would have to go over and over the same ground.

Once she jumped out of the window onto some scaffolding in order to get out of the house. She was later found in the home of a local heroin addict. I checked with CAPS whether it would be OK to put a lock on her window for her safety, but she broke the lock. Another time she stayed away for a couple of nights and was found at the local funfair. We were concerned about the company she was keeping, and for her own safety everyone agreed that it would be better if we all had a short break, so she went to respite with some other foster carers in the CAPS scheme. I took Joanne there myself because I wanted to explain to her en route that she was going for respite because of the risky situations she was putting herself into.

Her social worker brought her back to us for a meeting and we talked about what had happened. Joanne said she was really sorry and wanted to be with us. I think she was expecting us to reject her, so she'd have to be moved on again. I think us being prepared to take her back made a tremendous difference to our relationship with her. After she'd been with us about a year-and-a-half she started to settle down. With Joanne you had to let minor incidents go by and focus on the bigger things. We also knew what made her tick and the type of "carrots" you had to dangle to motivate her the right way. We came to recognise that she didn't seem to be able to behave at school and at home at the same time. If things were going well here, she'd probably have an outburst in class and be sent home or suspended.

Our local comprehensive couldn't take her but we'd got her a place in the local Catholic school. The guidance teacher was excellent and always tried to see things from our perspective. I don't think they'd ever had a pupil like Joanne before! They were pretty gob-smacked by the way she spoke to teachers and other children. One time she got into a fight and was about to hit the teacher who tried to break it up. The school was going to ban her for eight weeks but I think she'd have turned our house upside down. I kept her at home for two weeks and insisted she stay in her room and work during school hours, so she realised she wasn't getting an easy time. The headteacher, who was brilliant with Joanne, allowed her to go back after two weeks. Any longer and I think the placement would have come to an end!

I always let the school know I was available to pick Joanne up any time they needed me to, to prevent her from being suspended. They felt supported by that because they knew that I would then ground her when I got her home, so I was reinforcing the fact that her behaviour wasn't acceptable. She found it difficult to say when she didn't understand something in class and she'd disrupt the class rather than ask for help. I thought she was maybe having some problems with dyslexia but the school felt it was important to get her behaviour sorted out first. When they gave her some additional support she took a dislike to the teacher, making accusations of abuse, or she would constantly find reasons to avoid her and claim she'd forgotten the class. She did eventually get four standard grades in English, Hospitality, Home Economics and Art. I think she got that because I always insisted she went to school and stuck at her work. And I said that if she worked hard she could choose a reward. She said she'd really like a week's holiday abroad, and we kept this promise when she passed the exams.

As a child Joanne hadn't been allowed to attend her mum's funeral or be any part of the arrangements, which she had found very hard. She also had very little contact with her younger brothers who were also in care. She had an older sister, Mary, with whom she had a very superficial relationship. The most important relationship in Joanne's life was with her nana.

I'm one of ten brothers and sisters and I can't imagine what it must be like not to be able to pop round to your family whenever you want to. I tried to make sure that Joanne got regular contact with her younger brothers but the carers they were living with didn't seem to share my concerns. The children didn't seem to have a lot to say to each other, but Joanne really needed this contact and got upset when it didn't happen. So with the social worker I tried to get a rota together. We arranged that every six weeks all the children would meet at Mary's, the older sister's, house. The other carers often used to just not turn up and say they forgot. But I pushed and pushed to make sure it happened.

Joanne saw her nana every other weekend. And it was also a chance for her to see her friends in Perth, because this was where she'd grown up. It was Joanne's dearest wish that she could go back and live with her. But her nana was unwell most of the time. No one seemed to know what was wrong with her. Then her nana went into hospital and Joanne wasn't able to go to stay in Perth any more. Joanne felt very rejected that her sister, Mary, wasn't having her to stay at this time.

I felt that Joanne shouldn't miss out on the opportunities to be with her nana, and I took her regularly to visit her. I didn't want her to feel excluded, the way she had when her mother had died. As it became clear that her nana was about to die, the sister said Joanne could stay with her, but her nana lived for another fortnight. I was phoning Joanne three times a day and she knew she could phone at any time and I'd go and collect her. I'd also go over and take her out, because I didn't want her to be constantly exposed to the sadness of death. She had a fascination about death, due to being totally excluded from her mother's. Whenever a child at school had a death in the family, Joanne insisted on attending the funeral.

When her grandmother died, Joanne was relieved, excited and sad. She said she'd had this big fear about death, but she'd been there and had touched her nana. It had made it clear to Joanne what death was all about. It was something peaceful she didn't have to be scared of. We prepared her for the funeral, and a whole group of kids from her school came together with the headteacher who knew how important Joanne's nana was to her. Joanne handled it all very well – I think she realised she needed some calm time in her life. We could have very adult conversations with her at the time about her feelings. We could acknowledge that she felt angry and let down by her family, especially now the main person in her life had gone.

Joanne knew that her sister, Mary, wouldn't take her for regular weekends, so she'd lose that connection with her home and friends. We drew up a rota system with Mary so that Joanne would go once a fortnight and the brothers once a fortnight, so the sister would have two weekends every month to herself. Mary did try but it became more difficult for her. I think she had problems with her husband and she had small children of her own. Joanne felt a lot of rejection and couldn't believe she was only going to visit her home area about eight times a year.

At this time Joanne, who was now 15, started speaking about finding her dad, who it seemed had disappeared off the face of the earth. She'd always spoken about her father as if he was someone in the past, but now she started to talk about him in the present. As far as we knew, he was living rough in Perth. A social worker undertook the task of finding him. It seemed that Joanne's dad had AIDS and was a chronic alcoholic. Joanne's worker asked her father's worker to explain that his daughter wanted to see him. But the father responded by saying, 'I've already seen Joanne and she has a baby'. We knew that Joanne had a different dad from that of her older sister, Mary, so we were a bit confused by this. But he also said he didn't want to meet with his daughter at this stage.

We tried to put it into context for Joanne by comparing it with things that were happening in *Eastenders*, where a character had sores all over his legs and didn't want people to see him. I tried to explain it to her by saying, 'You've taken two years to think about whether you wanted to see your dad. Now he's going to need time to think about it too. It's been a shock to him, and he's ill and confused. Why don't you write a letter and the workers will pass it on.' Joanne said, 'I don't know if I do or don't want contact. Maybe I just want this because I feel I'm on my own in the world.' I thought it was good that Joanne was able to reflect on her feelings in that way.

Joanne decided not to write the letter. Then her dad was found dead. One of her dad's sisters rang up and painted a very rosy picture of him. Joanne had never heard good things about her dad before. I think Joanne was in shock. She was thinking about the fact that she would never get to see him. I have two relatives whose dad had died without them seeing him. I suggested that Joanne might like to talk to them about how they'd coped with this.

We went to the funeral and met some of these relatives she'd never known. There were a lot of alcoholic, dysfunctional people, including her dad's drinking buddies who were crying their eyes out. But it was a nice humanitarian service. Joanne's previous social worker also came with us, and it was good to have that extra support.

Then we met Joanne's other sister – the sister we didn't know she had! After the service one of the aunts invited us to join them at the pub and said, 'Do you know Gail?' And another aunt said, 'This is your sister'. Joanne had no idea she had a second sister. This sister had a small baby. We realised then that Gail must have been the person her dad was talking about, whom he'd confused with Joanne.

Gail was a daughter from another relationship. Gail knew Joanne existed but, because their dad was so confused, she'd thought her sister was about seven years old. And Gail had her own problems, she'd also been in the care system. But that day everyone promised Joanne the earth. Gail lived in Germany and was saying to Joanne, 'You can come and stay with us'. And all the relatives had nice stories to tell Joanne about her dad. Before that, all Joanne had was memories of her dad beating up her mum, and how much her nana hated her dad.

When we left, the aunts and uncles said they would be in touch. But we've never heard from any of them again and we've tried to make contact with them. Gail was in contact with Joanne on a fairly regular basis and they met up while Gail was in the country. Then Gail went back to Germany. She would email and the two of them phoned each other for a while. We were supportive of the idea of Joanne going to stay with Gail, but we felt she had to build up a relationship with her sister first. Gradually the contact fell away and they stopped phoning. Gail was expecting her second baby and she'd just lost one of her in-laws, so she had a lot of other things going on. But all this rejection made it a tough time for Joanne.

Joanne turned 16 around this time and it had always been a bit of a landmark for her. We made a big do of it but sadly no one from her family remembered. All through her time in care she had always been told that when you are 16 things will change – you will be able to make decisions. But nothing really changed in the way she was expecting, she didn't get that sudden freedom she was looking for. On top of which her other sister, Mary, said she couldn't have Joanne for Christmas. In the run-up to Christmas, she came home drunk six nights out of seven.

We made a real effort to try and make Christmas a special time and Christmas Day seemed to go well. On Boxing Day morning Joanne told me she'd had a nice time. But on Boxing Day night she lost it. She was going out and I said please don't come back drunk. But she came back very drunk and bedraggled. I had family round for a meal. I tried to persuade Joanne to go up to her room. She started swearing at me. I said, 'Calm down – you are scaring everyone'. I touched the small of her back with my arm to move her. She lost it completely and attacked me. She fell on the stairs and tried to kick and punch me. She then went out of the front door. She was outside screaming, saying she wanted to leave. A crowd of people started to gather to see what was happening. There were small children in the house and my sister, who was also Joanne's respite carer, explained to Joanne that she couldn't come back in again until she calmed down. I phoned the duty worker at CAPS and explained what was happening.

It was too late to find a respite place so I said, 'All I'm asking you to do, Joanne, is go to bed quietly tonight. If you really want to go then we'll talk about it in the morning.' Eventually she went to bed. She threw her stuff around a bit, but by midnight she was asleep.

In the morning I went and spoke to her. She said she wanted to leave and she insisted she hadn't been drunk. So it was decided she would go for a couple of day's emergency respite. Before this, everything had been focused on Joanne and how she felt. And this time I wanted her to understand how I felt about being attacked in my house. She spent three days with the emergency carers. She came back and said, 'I'm really sorry and I do want to be here. I'll go back to coming in at my normal times. I can't handle alcohol.' I said, 'That's fine, you can come back, but you really need to know how hurt I felt by your actions and what you said. As foster carers we are human and we have feelings, and sometimes you are over the top in your behaviour.'

For a little while Joanne managed without drinking. It was my birthday in February and I was going on a holiday my family had planned for me. My sister was going to look after Joanne while I was away. But Joanne came in streaming drunk the night before and started shouting again. She said, 'I'm going to cut my wrists so you won't be able to go on holiday'. She then left the house, and we were worried. We were up until three o'clock making calls to the police and NCH's on-call social worker. The police picked her up and she accepted that she needed to go for emergency respite. But Joanne persuaded the local authority duty social worker to let her go to her sister, Mary, for a few days.

Joanne was really keen on her freedom and I think that when she got to 16 and things didn't happen as she'd expected, she latched onto the idea that she could move out and go and live with her pals. She came back to us saying that she was grateful for everything we'd done for her but her social worker had found her a one-bed flat in an independent living scheme. I said, 'I don't blame you, I understand why you want this'. After that, the CAPS project gave her 28 days' notice – so she still had time to change her mind if she wanted to stay with us, and with CAPS.

Before she left, Joanne avoided us. I don't think she could handle being around us and knowing she was leaving. I went to give her a cuddle at one time and she backed off. She packed all her stuff and we drove her down to her new place. We didn't sleep for a week after that! I kept thinking, how on earth is she going to manage? I did ask her social work department to keep her bed with us open for two months. When I was 16, I had rebelled against my parents but still knew they were there for me. Just because Joanne is in care doesn't mean she shouldn't have that option of changing her mind if she wants to come back. They paid for her place to be kept open and she knew that. But I think for Joanne it would have been so hard to admit that she couldn't manage on her own. There was also the fact that she'd got her freedom and it was still "party-time" for her, some of the time!

When she moved, my professional hat said don't go and see her. My personal hat said I have to go! The first time I went down she was drunk – that was awful! But when I've visited since, her flat is usually tidy and she seems to be managing on the small amount of money she gets. She's also doing a course in independent living skills. I do worry though that she may need to go through the "drink and drugs" period before she really settles down and finds herself.

Joanne's social work department felt we'd done a very good job. Her social worker put in writing that I'd managed her behaviour very well, given her consistent boundaries and built up her self-esteem. They also felt I'd helped her deal with bereavement and relationships, and to keep in touch with her family. But you can't help feeling a bit sad when you feel things have ended on a rather sour note.

However, I still go and see Joanne about once a week and she's phoned me a couple of times. Sometimes when I knock at her door she doesn't answer, but I like her to know I'm still there for her. I tell her that our door is open if she needs us. She had a review meeting recently and her social work department hopes that she will stay in the area so that our family can continue to offer her support. We are really all she has so I hope, one day, she will feel she can come to us for Sunday tea.

| **An update:**

Therese added the following update to Joanne's story before this book went to print.

Joanne did go through the drink and drugs period I feared, and chose to lose contact with us. She also lost her placement at the supported accommodation and ended up homeless. However, we had always suspected she would go down the spiral of self-destruction before coming up the other end, as a stronger person.

I'm pleased to report that Joanne has since been in touch, claiming that for the past six months she has had no drink or drugs because she is now aware that she can't handle it. Joanne has now secured her own tenancy in our area and hopefully will continue her life here in Glasgow, with the support on offer from ourselves, my extended family and the community which has become her home.

Afterword

As these stories so clearly illustrate, many foster carers achieve the most amazing things. They live – 24 hours a day, seven days a week – with children and young people that many of us would find it hard to spend half an hour with. They take the brunt of sleepless nights, the criticism of strangers, the hurt of birth parents, and the confusion, anger and pain of the children and young people themselves. Unlike most of us, who retreat to the safety of our homes when the pressures of work become too much for us, their "work" is always with them.

This anthology shows that there are some highly talented, persistent and resilient foster carers, coming from all walks of life, and from all kinds of social and economic backgrounds. What all the carers in this anthology seem to have in common is that they are truly child-centred – prepared to go the extra distance, and prepared to hold on when things get tough. Yet they are also realists who do not look for magic solutions, or expect to have all the answers all of the time. They accept that some children and young people have had such a bad deal from life that they test, to the limits, the skills of even the most experienced carers.

These carers have a lot of wisdom to share with us, and throughout the book some helpful and poignant messages emerge, including these below.

Many carers speak of good relationships with their own agencies, but have often experienced difficulties working with the child or young person's social worker, who they feel could have offered more support or understanding of the individual child's needs. In some instances, carers say that they decided not to take children from a particular authority again because they believed the social worker's agenda was not sufficiently child-centred.

In several cases, carers speak of young people, and their birth families, making allegations against them. Although the carers expressed understanding of why children or adults make false allegations, and clearly appreciated the need to take complaints seriously, what they found most difficult to handle was the fact that, in most cases, the allegations were never properly resolved.

There are several cases in the book where carers have serious concerns about the circumstances in which children were returning home, and feel that nobody was giving due consideration to the child's wishes and feelings. As they were the people dealing with the child's anxieties on a day-to-day basis (for example, in the form of nightmares or endless questions about the future), they felt that sometimes the focus on reunifying families obscured the individual child's needs, especially when the child was younger or had difficulties vocalising their worries.

Several of the carers in this book worked with children who were preparing for "independent" living; yet, as their stories show, it can take considerable time and effort for a young person to move from a situation where their lives seem to be controlled by a number of outside forces – such as reviews, care plans and court orders – to a situation where they can fully function within society on their own. These carers show a very clear understanding that young people need space and support to make the "mistakes" that many young people make when they leave the family home for the first time. They are often the ones who are providing valuable (unpaid) support, many years after a placement has officially ended.

Several carers in this book express concern and sadness that they were no longer in touch with children with whom they had promised to be in touch. They worried that, having reassured the child that they would still be considered part of the family or would have some form of contact, the child was left feeling that, once again, their trust had been betrayed by adults they had become close to.

Foster carers may sometimes be seen as "too involved" to take a dispassionate overview of the situations they work with, but the value of their views should never be forgotten. They are, after all, the only ones with the detailed and intimate knowledge of living with an individual child around the clock.

Conclusion

Fostering children with very complex needs is not for everyone. However, for those able and prepared to develop the skills, energy and confidence to "stick" with these children, there are some very real emotional rewards. Perhaps what these stories show, more than anything else, is that there are no "stereotypical" foster carers. However incredible their achievements, these people are not a breed apart but normal human beings – from all walks of life – who have found something within themselves, that motivates, even compels them, to try and see the world through children's eyes, and to stick with them when the going is at its most tough. If this book encourages one new person to consider the skills they could bring to fostering in order to help some of our most troubled children, then something truly worthwhile has been accomplished.

Henrietta Bond

Useful organisations

British Association for Adoption & Fostering (BAAF)

BAAF is a registered charity and professional association for all those working in the child care field. BAAF's work includes: giving advice and information to members of the public on aspects of adoption, fostering and child care issues; publishing a wide range of books, training packs and leaflets as well as a quarterly journal on adoption, fostering and child care issues; providing training and consultancy services to social workers and other professionals to help them improve the quality of medical, legal and social work services to children and families; responding to consultative documents on changes in legislation and regulations affecting children in or at risk of coming into care; and helping to find new families for children through *Be My Parent*.

More information about BAAF can be obtained from our offices listed below.

Head Office
Skyline House
200 Union Street
London SE1 0LX
Tel: 020 7593 2000
Email: mail@baaf.org.uk
www.baaf.org.uk

Be My Parent
Address as Head Office
Tel: 020 7593 2060/1/2

BAAF England

Central and Northern Region
Grove Villa, 82 Cardigan Road
Headingley
Leeds LS6 3BJ
Tel: 0113 274 4797
Email: leeds@baaf.org.uk

and at:
Dolphin House
54 Coventry Road
Birmingham B10 0RX
Tel: 0121 753 2001
Email: midlands@baaf.org.uk

and at:
MEA House
Ellison Place
Newcastle-upon-Tyne NE1 8XS
Tel: 0191 261 6600
Email: newcastle@baaf.org.uk

Southern Region
Skyline House
200 Union Street
London SE1 0LX
Tel: 020 7593 2041/2
Email: southern@baaf.org.uk

BAAF Cymru
7 Cleeve House
Lambourne Crescent
Cardiff CF14 5GP
Tel: 029 2076 1155
Email: cymru@baaf.org.uk

and at
Suite C, 1st Floor
Darkgate, 3 Red Street
Carmarthen SA31 1QL
Tel: 01267 221000
Email: carmarthen@baaf.org.uk

and at
19 Bedford Street
Rhyl
Denbighshire LL18 1SY
Tel: 01745 336336
Email: rhyl@baaf.org.uk

BAAF Scotland
40 Shandwick Place
Edinburgh EH2 4RT
Tel: 0131 220 4749
Email: scotland@baaf.org.uk

Fostering Network

The Fostering Network is a membership organisation for everyone involved in fostering. It campaigns for higher standards of care for fostered children and young people, and gives support to fostering services and foster carers.

The Fostering Network provides a 24-hour legal advice service, runs training courses, and publishes a quarterly magazine, *Foster Care*, and a range of books for foster carers, social workers and other professionals.

Head Office
87 Blackfriars Road
London SE1 8HA
Tel: 020 7620 6400
www.fostering.net

The Fostering Network in Scotland
2nd Floor Ingram House
227 Ingram Street
Glasgow G1 1DA
Tel: 0141 204 1400

The Fostering Network in Northern Ireland
216 Belmont Road
Belfast BT4 2AT
Tel: 02890 673 441

The Fostering Network in Wales
Suite 11, 2nd Floor
Bay Chambers
West Bute Street
Cardiff Bay CF10 5BB
Tel: 02920 440 940

| **Other useful organisations**

Contact a Family

Provides support, advice and
information for carers of children with
disabilities, and helps to put families in
touch with each other.

209–211 City Road
London EC1V 1JN
Tel: 020 7608 8700
Helpline: 0808 808 3555

National Council of Voluntary Child Care Organisations

Offers information, training and advice
to voluntary child care organisations.
Individual supporters can subscribe to
their monthly news bulletin and
quarterly journal.

Unit 4, Pride Court
80–82 White Lion Street
London N1 9PF
Tel: 020 7833 3319

NCH

Works to improve the lives of
vulnerable children by offering a range
of services, including residential, foster
care and adoption services, leaving care
services and short break projects.
Produces a variety of leaflets and
information.

NCH England
85 Highbury Park
London N5 1UD
Tel: 020 7704 7000

NCH Cymru
St David's Court
68a Cowbridge Road East
Cardiff
CF11 9DN
Tel: 029 2022 2127

NCH Scotland
17 Newton Place
Glasgow
G3 7PY
Tel: 0141 332 4041

The Who Cares? Trust

Works to improve public care for
children and young people who are
separated from their families and living
in residential or foster care.

Head Office
Kemp House
152–160 City Road
London EC1V 2NP
Tel: 020 7251 3117

Who Cares? Scotland

Committed to improving the standard
of life for all looked after children and
young people in Scotland. The
organisation also works to raise
awareness of the problems affecting
young people who are or have been
looked after.

Who Cares? Scotland
Head Office
Oswald Chambers
5 Oswald Street
Glasgow
G1 4QR
Tel: 0141 226 4441

Children in Scotland

The national agency for voluntary,
statutory and professional organisations
and individuals working with children
and their families in Scotland. They
provide training, publications and the
monthly magazine, *Children in
Scotland*.

Princes House
5 Shandwick Place
Edinburgh
EH12 4RG
Tel: 0131 228 8484

Useful resources

| BOOKS FOR ADULTS

The books listed below are available from BAAF. Please visit www.baaf.org.uk or contact 020 7593 2072 for more details.

PARENTING

Caroline Archer, *First Steps in Parenting the Child who Hurts*, Jessica Kingsley Publishers, 1999

Caroline Archer, *Next Steps in Parenting the Child who Hurts*, Jessica Kingsley Publishers, 1999
These books offer practical, sensitive guidance through the areas of separation, loss and trauma in early childhood, and into adolescence. The effects of early emotional trauma are explained, and the author reviews specific sensitive situations that commonly arise.

Brian Cairns, *Fostering Attachments*, BAAF, 2004
This compelling book describes the unusual model of family group care undertaken by Brian and Kate Cairns, whose three birth children and 12 foster children lived together in their family home. Brian describes the benefits of family group membership in aiding learning and recovery for children who have had difficult pasts.

Kate Cairns, *Attachment, Trauma and Resilience*, BAAF, 2002
Draws on Kate's personal experiences with three birth children and 12 fostered children to describe family life with children who have experienced attachment difficulties, loss and trauma, and suggests what can be done to promote recovery and develop resilience.

Kate Cairns in conversation with John Simmonds, *Finding a way through*, BAAF, 2003
This passionate, inspirational and powerful video offers carers and parents who are striving to understand and heal children who have been damaged, ways of reaching out to them.

Vera Fahlberg, *A Child's Journey through Placement*, BAAF, 1995, reprinted 2004
Invaluable for all those involved in childcare, this book contains the theoretical knowledge base and skills necessary for understanding and working with children who are separated from their families. Comprehensive sections on attachment, separation and child development are included, all illustrated with case studies.

Stephen Hicks and Janet McDermott (eds), *Lesbian and Gay Fostering and Adoption*, Jessica Kingsley Publishers, 1998
This immensely readable book will be of great encouragement to lesbians or gay men considering fostering or adoption. It tells openly and honestly how it is, without resorting to jargon or becoming weighted down with politics.

Claudia Jewett, *Helping Children cope with Separation and Loss*, BAAF/Batsford, 1995
Using case histories and simple dialogues, this book details a range of simple techniques that adults can use to help children through their experiences of grief and loss.

Catherine Macaskill, *Adopting or Fostering a Sexually Abused Child*, BAAF/Batsford, 1991
This book describes the findings of a 1989 research project covering 80 placements of abused children. It discusses the implications for all involved, discussing how to help children talk through their experiences, and the impact on other children in the family.

FOSTER CARE STUDIES

Gillian Schofield, Mary Beek and Kay Sargent with June Thoburn, *Growing up in Foster Care*, **BAAF, 2000**
For a significant group of children, long-term foster care is their best chance of a secure family life. This research study follows 58 children, their foster carers, birth parents and childcare workers, looking at the impact of abuse, neglect and separation on the children's behaviour.

Mary Beek and Gillian Schofield, *Providing a Secure Base in Long-term Foster Care*, **BAAF, 2004**
This study records progress over three years of the group of children first met in *Growing up in Foster Care*, and describes how many of the children were beginning to relinquish some of their more troubled behaviours. First-hand accounts add depth and immediacy to the book.

Gillian Schofield, *Part of the Family: Pathways through foster care*, **BAAF, 2002**
Based on the stories of 40 young adults who were fostered long-term, the author describes the varied routes that children can take through foster care, looking at what made some experiences successful and others less so.

Moira Walker, Malcolm Hill and John Triseliotis, *Testing the Limits of Foster Care*, **BAAF, 2002**
This study looks at the pioneering Community Alternative Placement Scheme (CAPS), set up by NCH Action for Children in Scotland, highlighting how high-quality foster care can allow many children from secure care to remain in the community.

USEFUL GUIDES

Henrietta Bond, *Fostering a Child*, BAAF, 2004
This short, general guide to fostering in the UK will be an ideal starting point for anyone considering becoming a foster carer. It describes the children needing to be fostered; who can foster; who to approach if you want to apply; and how to get started.

Kate Cairns and Chris Stanway, *Learn the Child*, BAAF, 2004
A resource pack (containing a book and CD-ROM with a Powerpoint presentation) which looks at how foster carers, teachers and social workers can help looked after children to gain full benefit from their lives at school.

Robbie Gilligan, *Promoting Resilience*, BAAF, 2001
This pioneering book applies the concept of resilience to work with children in residential and foster care. Packed with practical ideas on how to improve the quality of life for children in care using relationship networks in their family, school and leisure activities.

Jayne Hellett with John Simmonds, *Parenting a Child who has been Sexually Abused*, BAAF, 2003
This skills development training programme for carers comprises five sessions which look at recognising abuse, how carers can help, and the role of therapy.

Selam Kidane and Penny Amerena, *Fostering Unaccompanied Asylum-Seeking and Refugee Children*, BAAF, 2004
This two-day course provides a comprehensive introduction to the issues, and will prepare carers for the complex task of looking after these children.

Rena Phillips (ed), *Children Exposed to Parental Substance Misuse*, BAAF, 2004
This anthology considers the psychological, social and behavioural impact on children exposed to parental substance misuse. Medical experts provide useful information on the effects of certain drugs and alcohol, and social work practitioners consider how best children can be helped.

Tony Ryan and Rodger Walker, *Life Story Work*, **BAAF, 1999**
This popular and practical guide is essential reading for anyone involved in life story work with children. Accessibly presented and attractively illustrated.

Advice Note, *Private Fostering*, **BAAF, 1998**
Aimed at those considering private fostering in England and Wales, this leaflet explains what it involves and provides guidance.

The two books listed below are available from Fostering Network. Please visit www.fostering.net or contact 0845 4589910 for more details.

All about Fostering, **Fostering Network**
Presented in a highly accessible, magazine-style format, this introductory guide answers the common questions people have when considering fostering. Personal experiences and opinions of existing foster carers, social workers and young people are included.

Becoming a Foster Carer, **Fostering Network**
An essential guide for people going through the assessment process to become foster carers, which sets out what happens during the stages of assessment.

| BOOKS FOR CHILDREN

The books listed below are available from BAAF. Please visit www.baaf.org.uk or contact 020 7593 2072 for more details.

Bruce's Multimedia Story, CD-ROM, Information Plus, 1998
Bruce's Multimedia Story raises issues about identity and change, capitalising on children's natural interest in computer-based activities. Animation, sound effects and music make the whole experience more productive for worker and child. Runs under Windows 3.1, Windows 95 or on Macintosh.

Hedi Argent and Mary Lane, *What Happens in Court?*, BAAF, 2003
A user-friendly guide to help children understand the role a court might have in their lives. Easily understandable and brightly illustrated.

Sheila Byrne and Leigh Chambers, *Feeling Safe*, BAAF, 1998
Tina has to go into foster care following abuse in the home.

Sheila Byrne and Leigh Chambers, *Waiting for the Right Home*, BAAF, 2001
Daniel is in short-term foster care, waiting to go home.

Jean Camis, *My Life and Me*, BAAF, 2001
This colourful and comprehensive life story book will help children living apart from their families develop and record memories of their past. Written by a social worker with extensive experience of direct work with children, *My Life and Me* is supplied with practice guidelines.

Jean Camis, *We are Fostering*, BAAF, 2003
Designed along similar lines to *My Life and Me*, this colourful and durable workbook will help birth children to know their history and role in the family, and prepare them to welcome foster brothers and sisters into their homes and lives.

Angela Lidster, *Chester and Daisy Move on*, BAAF, 1999
This popular and engaging picture book is for use with children aged 4–10 who are

moving on to adoption, to help them explore feelings about their past and their moves, and to help carers identify these issues from the child's perspective.

Barbara Orritt, *Dennis Duckling*, The Children's Society, 1999

Dennis, an appealing little duckling, has to leave his family as they can no longer look after him. He goes to live on a new pond where he begins to make new friends and is cared for by grown-up ducks. Suitable for use with children aged 4–8.

Shaila Shah, *Fostering: What it is and what it means*, BAAF, 2003

This is a short, brightly illustrated guide to fostering for children and young people, covering the different types of fostering, how children come to be fostered, parents, contact and many other questions. Designed to be worked through with a child before and during foster care.

The books listed below are available from Amazon. Please visit www.amazon.co.uk for more details.

Sharon Creech, *Ruby Holler*, Bloomsbury, 2003

Dallas and Florida live in the Boxton Creek Home, and have a reputation for rule-breaking and being "difficult to place". But the unconventional elderly couple who offer them a foster placement have a patient and unobtrusive approach to parenting which turns out to be just right. Suitable for children aged 10 and upwards.

Martina Selway, *So Many Babies*, Red Fox, 2003

Mrs Badger doesn't know what to do with her extra rooms until she reads that there are 'so many babies' who need her care. She starts with just one but ends up with so many children that she needs to build an extension. Told in rhyme and with the counting elements adding an additional bonus, this book is helpful for young children who are fostered.

Jacqueline Wilson, *The Story of Tracy Beaker*, Yearling Books, 1992
Tracy is ten years old. She lives in a Children's Home but would like a real home one day. Written as Tracy's diary, this is a lively, humorous book which reveals a lot of what goes on in the minds of children separated from their parents. Winner of several awards and adapted for television.

Jacqueline Wilson, *The Dare Game*, Yearling Books, 2001
The sequel to *The Story of Tracy Beaker*. Tracy is now settled in the home of her foster carer, Cam. Tracy had imagined everything would be perfect but finds this is not the case. When playing truant from school, she meets two boys also dealing with problems in their lives.

Jacqueline Wilson, *Dustbin Baby*, Yearling Books, 2002
Fourteen-year-old April was abandoned as a baby in a dustbin, and has since been through a failed adoption, a foster home, a children's home and a special school. But she is now able to find out who really cares about her. A highly readable account of the mixed emotions of an abandoned child, providing children and adults with insights about how it feels to be "in care".